A definite must-read for anyone healing from the loss of a marriage. Profoundly insightful, compassionate, encouraging, and provoking, Dr. Bacon's words will uplift you while allowing you to embrace your difficulties with hope.

As both a licensed psychologist and a marriage and family therapist, Dr. Bacon possesses acute clarity on the needs, issues, and struggles facing those who must navigate the treacherous terrain of divorce. Her expertise is second to none, yet her experience is what makes this book personal— deeply personal. While she lost her spouse to death, her husband Ron lost his spouse to divorce. Together they have demonstrated how God can, and indeed does, bring restoration from brokenness. Ron and Melody's story subtly weaves throughout this book. Their story, along with the many stories provided here, give the reader a sense of hope.

You will put down this book thinking, *Divorce can be filled with grace. It can be done. I can do it.*

—Andrew Stenhouse, EdD, director, industrial-organizational
psychology, Concordia University Irvine; author, *Broken:
A Guide Toward Emotional and Relational Restoration*

Despite our most fervent hope that divorces not occur in our communities and congregations, they do. And while our society is eager to support marriage, we often fail to invest the same measure of concern and care in supporting those whose marriages have failed. Dr. Melody Bacon should be commended for confronting this difficult issue squarely and offering guidance to help divorcing families progress through the period of disequilibrium, confusion, and uncertainty," to a place of emotional and spiritual wholeness.

—David Brill, author, *A Separate Place: A Family, a Cabin in the
Woods,* and *A Journey of Love and Spirit and As Far as the Eye
Can See: Reflections of an Appalachian Trail Hiker*

The title *The Grace-Filled Divorce* seems counterintuitive at first consideration. We have all witnessed the anger, blame, hurt, and devastation of divorce. Disappointment enters the breach once filled with love, trust, and hope for the future. Enormous emotional upheaval produces opportunities for extreme behavior. We're in a process of grief, whether we recognize it or not. The new journey to recover from grief—better, and not bitter—is a choice.

The Grace-Filled Divorce is an important resource on this journey toward health and wholeness. The book carefully outlines proven steps to recovery. The result of reading and applying this book will be evident, as your peace is restored and your relationships improved.

My life is a living example of the hard work of restoration. *The Grace-Filled Divorce* was a great tool in my recovery, and I recommend it for anyone seeking to recover from divorce.

—Robert S. Derryberry, DC, Paso Robles, CA

Often the Church needs to hear and receive the very message it is called to proclaim. The Gospel, it is said, is for the shipwrecked, for those who long for a word of healing and reconciliation. Sadly, the Church seems more "law" than "Gospel" and shuts its heart from those it judges to have failed. Melody Bacon challenges the Church with the Good News—not only on behalf of those of us who are divorced, but on behalf of all of us, teaching us what it is to live under grace.

—Alan Jones, dean emeritus, Grace Cathedral, San Francisco; honorary canon, Cathedral of Our Lady of Chartres; author, *Soul Making*

The Grace-Filled Divorce

The Grace-Filled Divorce

ALLOWING GOD TO REDEEM YOUR PAIN FOR THE GREATER GOOD

MELODY BACON, Ph.D.

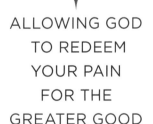

Deep River BOOKS

Published by
Deep River Books
Sisters, Oregon
www.deepriverbooks.com

ISBN-10: 1937756661
ISBN-13: 9781937756666

Library of Congress: 2012952248
Printed in the USA

Design by Robin Black, www.blackbirdcreative.biz

Acknowledgments

This book has been over a decade in the making, and many people have lived with it throughout the years. I am truly grateful to my children, Justin Kubassek and Mallory Bacon, for their love and support; they are both examples of God's redemption of grief in my life. I also want to express my gratitude to my parents, Vern and Audrey Christensen—to my dad for, among many other things, introducing me to the works of Carl Jung and to my mother for bequeathing me a love of literature. My sister, Tracy Grabin, has been a listening ear throughout the years as well as an enthusiastic supporter of my work. Her husband, Rick, and their children, Sean and Kelsey, have added much fun and laughter to my life. I want to thank my late husband, Alexander Kubassek, who taught me so much in the short time we had together—most particularly, that life should be lived to its fullest and that risk-taking is part of the adventure.

No book comes to fruition without the support and encouragement of many caring and giving individuals. And while it is not possible to thank everyone individually, please know that I am deeply appreciative. I want to thank Chuck Smith, Jr. for his wise words of counsel in this undertaking in addition to the very tangible expression in writing the foreword.

Lastly, I want to thank my husband and fellow traveler, Ron Bacon. His presence is my life has been a tangible sign of God's love and grace. His patience, humor, and playfulness have added much-needed balance. His quirky way of looking at things has helped in ways that are too numerous to count, and I know this book would not be the same without his insights. I count him among my life's greatest blessings.

Table of Contents

Foreword

At first glance, the phrase "grace-filled divorce" looked wrong to me. Grace-filled divorce is like describing an event as a "pleasant tragedy." Tragedy, by definition, is unpleasant. Where does one see any grace in the way divorce severs in two something that was meant to remain whole? To my mind—and personal experience—divorce is one of those terrible, life-destroying events that hammers the survivors with guilt and shame for many years afterward.

Bring this heartache into a Christian setting and you find it is compounded in churches that, despite what they claim to the contrary, continue to stigmatize both parties of a failed marriage. After all, with all the sermons, seminars, books, and other resources proffering biblical keys to a perfect marriage, how could anyone even speak of "Christian divorce"? Further, salt is rubbed into the wound in every formal wedding ceremony where we are reminded, "Those whom God has joined together let no one put asunder."

I used to be one of those evangelical pastors who was afflicted with chronic skepticism when it came to Christians who were divorced. Now it embarrasses me to admit I was always suspicious that divorced Christians had not tried hard enough, did not trust God strongly enough, or did not follow the Scriptures closely enough to keep their marriage together. Growing up with the deeply ingrained belief that marriage was forever, I naturally assumed the absolute permanence of my own marriage. The idea that I could one day be divorced simply did not occur to me. I assumed that my wife would always be my wife, the way that my parents were always my parents, my sisters were my sisters, and so on.

I have never believed or taught that a person should remain in an abusive marriage. Faced with domestic violence, some believers think they must tough it out because they have been told it is God's will. Others feel responsible as good Christians to maintain the image of the perfect little bride and groom balanced atop the wedding cake. But when there is no abuse and there has been no affair, when it is simply a matter of falling out of love or running into constant tension with one's spouse, it always seemed to me that if a couple sought the help of qualified counselors and gave their best effort to their marriage, together they could make it work.

My simplistic theory was blown apart when my first wife told me, "I'm convinced the only answer to our problems is divorce." I was not only stunned and confused, but her decision also threw me into the most agonizing grief and deepest depression I had ever known. Even now, it does not sound to me like I am exaggerating when I describe that season of my life by saying, "I went through hell." From the perspective of my own experience, divorce is the psychological equivalent of a car wreck that severely injures people, leaving them badly damaged in mind, body, and soul.

I could go on with a long list of all the suffering and hardships that follow a divorce—many of which are described well in the following pages—but my point is that in light of the normally misery-filled divorce, one naturally wonders how Melody Bacon can write about grace-filled divorce.

The answer lies in the wonderful and remarkable gift Dr. Bacon has given to people groping their way through the dark tunnel of divorce and to others who want to be a source of support, comfort, and healing to friends going through it—a process which generally lasts for two years, but in not a few cases stretches out for many more. Not for one moment does Melody dodge the truth of divorce, but unflinchingly probes the depths of its horror and ugliness. At no point does she pretend divorce is a wonderful experience. Nor does she merely promise her readers a life after divorce. Instead, the beauty of her wise insight and counsel is that, as she walks the path of divorce with us, she reveals its potential for spiritual growth. She shows us that God does not let all this pain and heartache go to waste. Rather, she uses it to help us identify with Jesus in His suffering, to forge stronger and more lasting bonds with the important people in our lives, and to discover our true selves.

But spiritual growth has never been easy. Many people who are divorced choose the less painful and difficult option of anesthetizing themselves by jumping into a new relationship. The instant relief of this option is transient and totally ineffective when it comes to healing the broken soul. Healing takes time, some education, and a lot of effort. For that reason, a radical difference can sometimes be observed in couples five or ten years after their divorce. The ones who avoided the pain of learning the lessons of divorce remain the same (frequently shallow) people they had always been, while the wisdom and maturity of those who have worked at understanding themselves as well as the breakdown of their marriage—and sought to change—are obvious. Those who have grown have simply become more interesting people than those who stagnate.

Dr. Bacon provides us an excellent overview of specific areas of our lives where we can focus our attention if we intend to grow through divorce. She also provides training exercises for developing necessary skills for recovering our lives and forming healthy relational bonds with other people. Through the case histories she shares with us, she takes us into the heart of the storm, illustrates the breakdown of our attitudes, beliefs, and behaviors, and then shines a light on the path we need to follow to progress toward the goals that matter most.

I am grateful to Melody for allowing me to write this foreword, because I have something to say to Christians who are divorced: Regardless of what anyone tells you, the Lord Jesus Christ does not see you or treat you as a second-class citizen in the kingdom of God. It would require another book to explore the ways we western Christians have misread Jesus' teaching, that "anyone who divorces his wife, except for sexual immorality, makes her the victim of adultery, and anyone who marries the divorced woman commits adultery" (Matthew 5:32). Suffice it for now to note that Jesus was shutting down a practice of legitimizing adultery through divorce on specious grounds. Nor is this the place to go into the possibility that God's "I hate divorce" statement in Malachi 2:16 (NLT) most likely refers to the cavalier way Ezra forced Jewish men to divorce their non-Jewish wives.

When we look into the Old Testament law, Moses not only permitted divorce, but there are also commandments that indicate it was assumed divorce was not uncommon (e.g., Leviticus 21:7, in which only priests were prohibited from marrying divorced women). Moreover, the Law anticipated instances of divorce and remarriage (Deuteronomy 24:1–4), and at least two statutes remove a man's right to divorce his wife as punishment (Deuteronomy 22:19, 29).

My recommendation is that if the culture and people of the church you attend treat you as though you are less of a Christian for being divorced, or they give you the impression you are unfit for the service to which God has called you, you find a new church. Unfortunately, marriage is not the only institution where abuse regularly occurs. A complete healing of your person is greatly enhanced when you are a member of a healthy community that embraces you in the love of God and for who you are. The people who make up that kind of community are the ones with whom you want to walk, grow, and spend eternity.

—Chuck Smith, Jr.

PREFACE

Divorce, if it were rightly done, would be done
as an act of love and done for the honest good
of the people involved. Such divorce, though rare,
remains nonetheless possible and may be necessary.

—DALLAS WILLARD
The Divine Conspiracy

This book has been almost a decade in the making. It began with my dissertation research on grief in divorce, which itself was begun earlier during my doctoral studies as I explored the topic of grief from different perspectives. When I completed work on my dissertation I was convinced that I would publish a book based on my research within a year or two. But the vicissitudes of life—internship and licensing, building a private practice, teaching, and raising a family—seemed to get in the way.

I worked on the book off and on, making one start and then another during those years. Finally about four years ago I wrote a book proposal with the help of a talented and encouraging writing coach, Cindy Barrilleaux, and I was convinced I was well on my way to publication. At that time, I resisted writing a book that would be categorized as a "Christian" book. For one thing, I wanted to reach a larger audience, much like I do in my private practice. In addition, having presented workshops on various topics at churches over the years, I was aware that this audience can be harshly critical. Thus, like Jonah, I ran in the opposite direction, away from Nineveh, motivated by much the same reasons—mainly fear, I suspect.

I feared that people who identified as Christians would not find this book to be "Christian" enough; I feared that those who aren't Christians would find it to be too religious. But mostly, I feared the condemnation of fellow believers who would see this book as advocating divorce. Of course, nothing could be further from the truth. Anyone who has sat for hours with hurting individuals suffering through a divorce, or who has endured the pain of divorce themselves, could not truthfully say that divorce is the good choice, even though at times it is the better of two miserable alternatives.

So I began to write the book based on a book proposal that avoided too much "spiritual" emphasis and focused on ideas from relational psychology. But as I wrote, and almost completed the book, I discovered a kind of deadness within myself. I did not have the enthusiasm for the writing. I found myself writing, as it were, with one arm tied behind my back. Finally, I realized that I had lost my way. I needed to write what I felt God was calling me to write—what my own spirit wanted to say—to rediscover the depth and meaning of this work. Beyond that, I knew that I wanted to blend the ideas of spiritual formation, the practices of ancient Christianity, with my research on the journey of grief through divorce. This was the book I wanted to write; this was the book I believe I was called to write.

This process—hearing a call, resisting that call, and finally answering the call—is a mirror image of the process of spiritual formation in general. It is a story that has been lived out many times over the centuries and seems to be a common response of human beings to the impress of the Divine on our lives. Whether out of pride, stubbornness, fear—or all of the above—we seem to struggle initially with cooperating with the Holy Spirit in conforming our lives to the life of Christ, which is the goal of spiritual formation.

The Grace-Filled Divorce holds as its primary premise that suffering is a means by which God can use us to become Christ to a hurting world. This is as true of divorce as it is of other experiences of loss; and yet, because of a variety of complex sociological, psychological and theological issues, grief in divorce has not been given adequate recognition. The truth is that despite its relative prevalence, divorce—much like abortion—is a subject that lies in the shadows of the Christian community. And, like abortion, it is an experience that carries with it not only loss and grief, but also deep shame, guilt, and feelings of failure.

I also believe that divorce does not have to be conducted in the way that is so commonly the case today. Divorce does not have to be the battle cry that commences with the hiring of attorneys and ends with survivors who walk off the field of war, limping and bleeding. Like Dallas Willard, I believe that divorce can be rightly done, so that damage is mitigated. In order for this to happen, a person needs a "listening ear"—someone who is willing to listen for the still, small voice of God in the midst of the chaos and confusion that are a part of the grief in divorce. That, too, is an aim of this book: to assist the reader in quieting down and opening up to the work of God during a very challenging time of life.

If Jesus were to come back today, I know He would associate with the divorced, as well as all the marginalized, wounded people who do not feel comfortable in church. I say this because this is what He did during His time on earth. It is my hope this work will carry on, in some small way, the work that Jesus began, bringing comfort to those who need comfort, hope to those who need hope, and grace to those who need grace.

INTRODUCTION

The longest journey is the journey inward.

—DAG HAMMARSKJÖLD

Call the world if you please "The vale of Soul-making."

—JOHN KEATS

Every experience of transformation begins with a journey. "In the middle of the journey of our life, I came to my sense in a dark forest, for I had lost the straight path," writes Dante at the beginning of *The Divine Comedy*. Thus began for him a strange, wondrous, and often fearful, expedition that eventually led to an experience of the divine.

You may be in the midst of a dark forest in your life as you struggle with the experience of divorce. And you may find it strange to think of divorce as the beginning of a journey since it is most often associated with endings. Stranger still is the thought that this journey could lead to a deepening of your experience of God. Yet history is full of such unwanted expeditions. The wilderness wanderings of the Jews in their journey to the Promised Land, the aimless and painful youthful experimentations of St. Augustine, and the grief and suffering of everyday men and women all attest to the truth that it is often the unexpected and unwanted experiences of life that propel us into a shift of awareness. And it is only in hindsight that we can see how these adventures and challenges served to shape and refine us in ways that were unimagined.

This is what William Least Heat-Moon discovered in his travels along the blue-colored roads on the highway maps. Beginning his expedition in the wake of a failed marriage and a lost teaching position, he decided to explore the less-traveled blue highways around the United States. As he explains, "I took to the open road in search of places where change did not mean ruin and where time and men and deeds connected."[1] What he found along the way was a different sense of himself: "I can't say, over the miles, that I had learned what I wanted to know because I hadn't known what I wanted to know. But I did learn what I didn't know I wanted to know." [2]

This book is, in part, a collection of stories from people who have learned what they didn't know they wanted to know. Like William Least Heat-Moon, and perhaps like you, they began their expeditions after a failed marriage, though the journeys they took were along the blue highways within themselves. They represent the many individuals I have encountered in my practice as a psychologist who have decided to follow the road less traveled and courageously ventured forth through uncharted territory.

Perhaps the most surprising discovery each of these individuals made is that they developed a deeper, richer more nuanced experience of God. This is what I have observed in my work as well: God shows up in the least expected places and at the most unexpected times. So when a client comes to me in confusion and despair, I know that this is an opportunity for the divine to enter in and together we can see the places where God's presence has been revealed. Whether or not my client has a conscious religious faith, I believe, as Carl Jung once said, that "bidden or unbidden, God is present." Something greater than either my client or myself is about to make itself known in my client's life.

This book in particular focuses on how God reveals Himself in the journey of grief in divorce. I fully embrace the notion so beautifully described by John Keats, that this life is the "vale of soul-making." Seen in this light, the experience of grief in the aftermath of divorce can be recognized as an opportunity for spiritual formation, a chance to learn and grow in multiple ways—emotionally, psychologically, and spiritually.

But, as is so often the case in the things of God, you must make the decision to embrace this opportunity. The fact is that divorce places you at a crossroads—a choice between the wide, well-traveled road of avoidance or the less crowded and often unrecognized path through grief. This is where you stand, now thrust into a choice between two pathways: the familiar road (filled with divorce attorneys, courtroom custody battles, and winner-loser mentality) or the road less traveled (through grief, toward self-discovery and a deeper, more meaningful relationship with God).

Most people choose the first option. As soon as a divorce is decided upon, people are exhorted by well-meaning friends and family to run to the nearest divorce attorney. Anxiety and fear can be so heightened that the divorce quickly descends into a journey into hell. But it doesn't have to be this way. You can join the company of those individuals who are willing to buck the status quo and avoid this scenario by fully grieving the loss of the marriage and the end of the hopes and dreams that it contained. For you, grief could become the catalyst for a new life. As one of my contributors declared, "When I look back at where I have come from and the person I used to be, it still amazes me. That's all I can say. It still amazes me."

How do you get from grief and loss to amazement and wonder? That is what this book will teach you. With the tradition of spiritual formation as the underlying theme, you will learn, step by step, how to navigate the challenges of grief in divorce and how to identify the still, small voice of God along the way. In addition you will find chapters that explore the multiple facets of the divorce experience: the emotions of grief, shame, and guilt, the process of self-discovery, and the challenge of relating to your ex-spouse. Each chapter features a lesson highlighted in a sidebar with activities that will address the relational, psychological, and spiritual aspects of grief in divorce.

As a professor of psychology, I often tell my students that you can't take a person down a path you haven't been willing to go yourself. Though as psychotherapists we are certainly not obligated to have experienced everything our clients face, we have to have the courage to face our own measure of suffering, whatever that may be. In that way, the road through suffering can be seen as the task for every human being. As one of my own professors used to say, "We need to teach our clients to tolerate suffering." By that he meant that a great deal of needless emotional pain comes from trying to avoid true suffering, sometimes turning to all forms of distraction—drugs, alcohol, work, relationships—as a result.

But that only compounds the pain in our lives, and instead of moving through suffering to a transformed life, we end up in an endless cycle of chronic emotional pain. Conversely, having the courage to move through the pain of grief and loss may initially seem more difficult, but it is far more rewarding in the long run.

My Journey

My own experience of grief and suffering began with the death of my first husband. Even after twenty-one years have passed, I can clearly recall the last time I saw him. I sat in a hospital room and held his hand. It was cool and slightly damp. He lay in a light drug-induced coma, softly breathing while his sisters and I sat with him. He was thirty-six years old and dying of cancer.

We had been married for twelve years and had been blessed with the birth of our first child, a son, only ten months before. Neither of us could believe he was dying, and I know, as I felt his hand in mine, that I desperately wanted him to live. It was very late, close to ten o'clock at night, and I had to leave. I pressed his hand and told him I was going, and I asked him to press my hand if he understood. He did. It was the last communication we would have together. At four o'clock the following morning, he breathed his last. And thus began for me a descent into the underworld of grief and pain that would last for several years.

With the death of my husband, I was thrust into a direct encounter with the shadow-side of love. W. H. Auden beautifully expresses the tenor of this experience in his poem, *Funeral Blues*. "The stars are not wanted now: put out every one; pack up the moon and dismantle the sun; pour away the ocean and sweep up the wood; for nothing now can ever come to any good."[3] Having lost the one who was my "working week and my Sunday rest," I could see no reason for the world to go on.

Though the end of my marriage occurred through death, much of what I experienced is common to everyone who has loved and lost. In our modern-day culture, divorce is much more common than death in the dissolution of a marriage, yet however it occurs—through death or divorce—the end of the love brings grief and pain. This is compounded by the fact that the experience of love brings with it the promise of eternity. "I thought love would last forever," writes Auden as he highlights the deep sense of betrayal we feel at the loss of love.[4]

He might have also written, "I thought I would last forever," for that is what lies at the heart of this betrayal by love, the knowledge that just as love dies, we will die, too. In our grief, then, as we face the betrayal of the promise of love, we come face to face with our own finitude.

This is not only because we are confronted with the limitations of love itself, but also because in many ways, when the person we love most dies, or leaves us, or we leave them, we die, too. Life as we have known it will never be the same, and for what seems an eternity afterward, we will walk on this earth as though we were the living dead.

When we are in this state, we share something in common with the characters that Anne Rice writes about in her fictional works on vampires. In her book, *The Queen of the Damned*, she describes the longing of the vampire Pandora for her former life as a living person: "And as always happened in such moments, the vague shining human past she clung to seemed more than ever a myth to be cherished as all practical belief died away. That I lived, that I loved, that my flesh was warm."[5] When one is in the throes of grief, particularly in the early days, one feels as though the experience of love and warmth is a distant memory. Like the characters in Anne Rice's novels, we move among the living like the undead.

Certainly this was true of my experience. I recall few details of those early days of widowhood. It was as though I had died and my body continued to move among the land of the living. Now, when I try to remember details of those days, I can only grab hold of images, like photographs in an album, rather than a narrative that might add form and substance to the story contained therein.

I look back and see myself at the big farmhouse where I stayed with Alex's brother's family shortly before the funeral. I see myself sitting in the funeral parlor as people came to pay their last respects, looking at Alex's body and thinking, *He isn't there. His body is there, but he is gone.*

I see myself at the grave site, watching as they lower his casket into the ground. I see myself lying in the big bed back at the farmhouse where he and I had slept only a few short months before on a visit to his family.

Mostly, I recall my morning ritual in the days and months that followed. I would awaken and think, *Now, I will get up and place my feet on the floor. I will walk and attend to Justin.* That was as far ahead into the future as my mind could comprehend. To think of hours or days later was difficult; to imagine months or years ahead was impossible. My future, which had once contained all my hopes and dreams, had been destroyed. Now I faced a dark, incomprehensible void. *How,* I wondered, *will I ever live without him?*

After a while, life began slowly to seep back into the numbness that characterized my existence. I continued to care for my son. I participated in a playgroup we had begun before my husband's illness. I continued to attend various meetings of groups I was involved with. These all helped to keep me tied to the land of the living. Eventually, I sought out the help of a professional counselor with whom I could share the depths of my suffering. This was extremely valuable for me since I felt the freedom to explore some of the nameless fears that plagued me.

In particular, I struggled with the fear that I had lost my faith in God. I wasn't particularly aware of being angry with God, though I'm sure that was true. Rather, I was afraid that my relationship with Him had been permanently broken. I felt utterly alone in the universe, thrust into the outer darkness. I could not sense God's presence in my life.

I looked forward to my sessions with my therapist. They offered a time of relief from the vast aloneness that characterized my existence. I recall a time when I was returning from a gathering of friends, shortly before Alex's death. It was nighttime, and as I drove home alone, through neighborhoods that felt at once strange and familiar, I was struck by the aptness of the metaphor they presented. For there in the darkness, lights shone from the windows. Inside those houses, it seemed there was life and warmth; outside, it was dark and lonely. I remember thinking, *Now I am on the outside, looking in.* And that is how my life seemed for several years after Alex's death. Not all the time, but often enough. So for those few moments when I was with my therapist, and later with close friends, I was on the inside, and the darkness of the void was kept at bay.

It was not only the darkness that seemed to descend upon my life, but also the quietude. Evenings in particular seemed lacking in the sounds that fill up the spaces. After my son was in bed, the silence seemed to engulf the house. Before love left, I lived in the illusion of eternity. Now I was forced to confront its opposite—nonexistence, the end of time—and the world became empty and silent.

D. H. Lawrence writes so eloquently of this haunting silence:

> Since I lost you, I am silence-haunted;
> Sounds wave their little wings
> A moment, then in weariness settle
> On the flood that soundless swings.[6]

When love departs, we are left with a solitary, silent existence. This, for me, was a terrifying experience, but one that nothing could really assuage. Though the terror did not overwhelm me, it was there, nonetheless. The fear was that this is truly the essence of life and all else is an illusion.

In time, life took on a degree of familiarity once more. I remember a day, early in my widowhood, when I awoke with more energy than I had had since Alex's death. I cleaned my house; I cooked a complete meal for dinner. It was the first glimmer of hope that there might be a future for me, that perhaps I might rejoin the land of the living—not as an onlooker, but as an active participant.

Though the trajectory of my emergence out of the grief was not a straight one, it was a forward movement nevertheless. After about a year and a half I began to consider dating again. I was past the initial throes of grief, and I had begun to consider a plan for building a future for myself. Slowly, I was relinquishing the feeling of being married and I began to think of myself as a single woman.

This, too, presented a grief. While I was actively mourning, I still felt tied to my husband. It was as though the feelings of grief and sadness allowed me the illusion of continuity. I was still Alex's wife as long as I mourned. To acknowledge my singlehood was also to say "good-bye" to a part of me that had lived for most of my adult life, the part that was Alex's wife. To begin dating meant that I had to continue my farewell to Alex; it required that I loosen one more tie to my former existence. It was a difficult time for me, fraught with ambivalence and uncertainty. During this time of transition, I was not who I once was, and not yet who I would become.

Gradually, I began to have friends who were also single. Before my widowhood, all of my friends were married. One or two of my married friends got divorced; I met another who had never been married. I began to attend groups that were comprised of single adults. My greatest desire was to find happiness as a single person, to see how I could create a life of fulfillment outside of marriage.

At the same time, I was convinced that this was impossible. The whole world, it seemed, was married. I felt like a misfit as a single where everyone moved in pairs. "I feel like I'm living in Noah's Ark!" I used to complain.

It seemed this was particularly the case at church, where adult single activities were at best a poor stepchild to the family-focused activities of the church, and at worst, an embarrassment that the church was not sure how to handle. The vast majority of single adults my age were divorced, and this is a topic that the Christian community has yet to come to terms with effectively. Single adults do not represent the ideal of American Christian culture; they remind us that the ideal of marriage for life is not a reality for many people.

Because of this, I found that the church I had attended no longer felt like home. It no longer seemed appropriate to continue to be active in the married couples group, and the singles group, though once quite vibrant, was at an ebb. In addition, I found that my theology required a different style of worship, so I searched and found another church home. Even there, I was often painfully reminded of my awkward status. I remember attending a church family picnic with my then two-year-old son. It was a large gathering, and the few friends I had at the church were not in attendance, so Justin and I sat together on a blanket, surrounded by families.

And so it went, slowly—at times painfully. I was constructing a new life for myself and my son. Because he was only 10 months old when his father died, I do not know how it was for my son then. I can only imagine how confusing it was and that the loss of his father was painful at the time and will continue to be so in some ways throughout his life. Justin loved to be with people, and I know it was very difficult for him when we would leave to go home from a visit with friends. The tantrums he threw were monumental. To leave the energetic aliveness of a house full of people to return to the quiet of our house must have felt dreadful to him. I knew I could never be a father to him; I knew, too, that I would be the best mother I could be.

Through the years, I explored career possibilities, finally settling on academia as a historian. I began a part-time graduate program in American history at the local university and found a great deal of enjoyment in that endeavor. I honed my writing skills during that time, working with one professor in particular who insisted I rewrite papers until she could grant them an "A." This was a great gift to me and resulted in my receiving several awards for papers I had written as well as having one accepted for publication in an academic journal.

My work in the graduate program was significant in moving me closer to my initial goal. I found a great deal of happiness and fulfillment in my work. I made friends in the program who were like-minded and with whom I could share ideas over coffee or the occasional dinner out. I felt God's hand in my life once more. Life seemed to be opening itself up to me again.

In addition, I had also begun to explore the writings of Carl Jung. I attended lectures at the Jung Institute and read extensively within the field of Jungian psychology. This helped me to come to a different understanding of myself and my life. I recorded my dreams; I wrote in a journal. I wondered and explored and prayed. This, in turn, affected my writing of history and how I understood the events and activities of the lives of people, both past and present. My life was richer and deeper as a result.

In the midst of all this, I experienced what I call my "Bluebeard" relationship, after the story related by Clarissa Pinkola Estes in her work, *Women Who Run with the Wolves.*[7] It is about a naive young woman who marries a man, Bluebeard, despite her initial intuition that something is wrong. It is a story of danger and discovery, of growth and initiation.

My "Bluebeard" experience occurred in the context of a serious relationship with a man who was dangerous in an emotional and psychological way. It was an initiatory experience for me, albeit an extremely painful one. I learned a great deal about myself, about human nature, and the intrinsic feel of psychopathology.

I came close to marrying this man and can only claim God's grace for not having done so. This, too, was a gift. I gained insight into how deceptive a relationship can be, how hard it is to remain clear and true in the throes of romance, and how difficult it is to stand firm in one's position when it is continually being questioned and refuted. At times I felt like Alice in Wonderland; all sense of truth and reality was open for debate.

I came out of this relationship with much more clarity and confidence in remaining true to myself above all else. I remember that I finally understood that the worst experience was not to be alone, as I had once imagined, but to be in a relationship and feel so incredibly lonely. Suddenly, being single looked good. I broke off the relationship soon after that, and though there were times of ambivalence and wondering if I'd made a mistake, I held fast and continued my journey alone, but forever changed.

I moved forward in my graduate work toward a master's degree in American history and continued to be active in other areas of my life. I recall one evening settling down on my couch with a good book and thinking, *If I were to get seriously involved with another man, he would have to really add to all that I have.* My life was good. I remarked to my therapist that I believed I had come as close to creating a fulfilling and good life as I could as a single person. I still wanted eventually to remarry, but if I didn't, that would be all right. "That would be icing on the cake," I explained. "But even if I don't meet anyone, I've got the cake, and it tastes good."

A little over a year later I met the man who would become my husband. He has indeed added to my life in ways I never could have imagined. And yet, though he is a very important part of my life, he is not the sum total. My work, which has now changed to the field of depth psychology, continues to call me. God moves through my life in ways that are surprising at times. Having gone through the winter of bereavement, the "dark night of the soul," I have emerged with a stronger sense of myself and my calling. Through the alchemical vessel of grief and singlehood, I have been transformed.

The Grace-Filled Divorce is designed to help you face your grief in order to transform your life. It is written to help you learn how to eliminate resentment and bitterness by fully grieving the loss of your marriage, and in so doing, create a more positive relationship with your ex-spouse, your children, and ultimately yourself. Your willingness to travel the road through grief will empower you to move forward, unencumbered by the past—to embrace a new life. This is the pathway that lies before each divorcing individual. It is the journey from loss to transformation that comes from discovering the grace-filled divorce.

1. If you haven't done so already, purchase a blank book to use as a journal as you read through this book. Then, set aside some time to write down your story. How did you meet? What made you decide to get married? When did you become aware something was wrong? What efforts did you make to address the issues? When did you know you were going to divorce? How did you handle the news? Write this in a narrative form as though you were telling this story to a close and trusted friend.

2. Read the parable of the rich ruler in Luke 18:18–30. Before you read, ask the Holy Spirit to highlight for you a word or a phrase. Take your time and allow the words to sink in. Then, read it a second time and this time respond to God's prompting. It may come in the form of a new insight about yourself; it may manifest as a new understanding about God. Meditate on this and then pray for wisdom to respond to the insights you have gained in this exercise.

CHAPTER ONE

When Things Fall Apart: Laying the Groundwork

Unfurl the sails and let God steer us where he will.

—Bede

"Four springs have come and gone with their lilac mementos of my wedding, and Easter Sundays to remind me of the desperate time when things flew apart," writes Susan Spano in *Women on Divorce*, her words an echo of William Yeats, in his poem about the end of the world, "Things fall apart; the center cannot hold."[1]

This is the experience of divorce—it is the chaos of a dying world. Your old life is over; your new life has not yet begun, and what follows is a time of disequilibrium, confusion, and uncertainty.

Whether or not you wanted your divorce, the early days are the most challenging. Grief over the loss of something you once valued above all else thrusts you into a tumult of emotions that make it difficult to maintain your bearings. In addition, you feel as though you are in limbo, no longer married, and not yet settled into life after your divorce.

This is what has been called an experience of "liminality," a sacred space that opens us up to an encounter with God. The word comes from the Latin word *limen*, which is the space that exists underneath a threshold—when you stand there you are neither in one room, nor in the other. It is an unsettling space in which we can lose our bearings; as a result, we often experience this as frightening.

Ironically, this occurs at the most crucial time of divorce when you are asked to make decisions that can affect your life for years to come. Added to this is the fact that divorce brings with it a multitude of emotions—grief, shame, guilt, and uncertainty.

Despite its prevalence, divorce resides in the shadows of our culture. Like death, divorce is something we all acknowledge intellectually but prefer not to think about; it belongs in the realm of "it will happen to someone else." So it is little wonder that when it does occur, divorce strikes hard. All the hopes and dreams you held when you walked down the aisle on your wedding day are now dashed upon the rocks.

Needless to say, divorce is a complicated experience, clouded with assumptions of choice and failure. It is similar to suicide: Someone makes a decision to leave, but instead of a body, a marriage is killed. Yet, even in the aftermath of a suicide, those who are left behind are offered care and support. Covered dishes are brought to the bereaved; a funeral or memorial service is held. Grief is a shared communal experience.

But those who are divorcing are usually forced to go it alone—to grieve in private and navigate the turbulent emotional climate on their own. It seems that there is more compassion for those who lose a marriage through death than divorce.

This leaves divorcing individuals with far less emotional support to help them through this passage, despite the fact that it is far more perilous in many ways than widowhood. Most of us have seen the destructive potential of divorce, the decade-long custody battles, the tens of thousands of dollars spent on attorneys, the emotional and psychological trauma of accusations of sexual abuse and alcohol addiction that get tossed around like hand grenades. At its worst, the journey through divorce is like going through a war zone, air raid sirens blaring overhead, bombs detonating, you and your children ducking for cover.

This was the experience of one of my clients who spent two years in a contentious battle with her now ex-husband. Her attorney-driven anxiety propelled her into one skirmish after another—first over who stayed in the house (he did), then over who got the proceeds from the division of their assets (the attorneys did), and finally, the daily details of custody and visitation in which everyone is the loser.

Eventually, my client realized that divorce does not have to be this way, and she learned that it is possible to navigate the terrain of divorce with thoughtful intention. She and I worked together to determine the best responses based on her most deeply held values and principles. Most significantly, even when my client was in the throes of tremendous anxiety and fear, we were able to see God's presence, grace notes in the kindness of friends who offered her a listening ear, in the times of quiet evenings with her children in their small rental home, and in the possibilities that she and I both knew lay at the end of her tumultuous journey.

Over time, my client was able to let go of the ego-driven behavior that caused her to see this divorce as a fight, to stop the old habits that impelled her to react to her ex-husband out of anger and frustration, and instead, slowly begin to let go of her old attitudes and behaviors. Today my client's life is very different. Her relationship with her ex-husband is manageable; she has begun training for a new career and is embracing the new life that is opening up before her. She understands how God used the past two years as a time of spiritual formation, to assist her in finally releasing the firm grip she had on her old approach to life and instead move forward toward the life she has always dreamed of.

Grief in Divorce: An opportunity for personal growth and spiritual formation

What my client learned, and what you can, too, is that allowing yourself to fully experience the grief of divorce opens up a tremendous opportunity for growth in all areas of your life—most particularly, in the spiritual aspect. Loss, grief, and suffering have long been recognized by spiritual traditions as an opportunity for an encounter with God. St. John of the Cross called this "the dark night of the soul," when one feels abandoned by everyone, even God. Another name for this experience is a "night sea journey." Think of Jonah and his three days in the belly of the great fish.

No one seeks out these experiences and yet they come to everyone nevertheless. These dark nights often bring with them a sense of being abandoned by our friends, our loved ones, our community, and most especially God. Questions spring to mind: "How could this be happening to me?" "Why did God allow this to happen?" Like Jesus' cry on the cross, we are brought to the depth of despair, "My God, my God, why hast thou forsaken me?"

In the midst of one's darkest hour, however, lies the seeds of a new existence. St. John of the Cross asserts that the soul needs this time to mature, to move from a childlike relationship to God into a more fully developed, mature attitude. Keep in mind that Jesus' darkest hours were just before the resurrection. As Jesus explained, a seed must die in order for new life to emerge. Each experience of new life is preceded by a death. Though at times you may feel overwhelmed and discouraged, you can actively cooperate with this process and, together with the Holy Spirit, redeem this time of grief and loss. By working through the exercises in this book, you will be taking an important step in that direction.

The first step is to start each chapter with a prayer that the Holy Spirit will reveal to you what it is you need to learn. As you begin an exercise, pray for wisdom, insight, and peace. If you find that an exercise or suggestion is too difficult, set it aside and read the next chapter. You can always come back to it later. Timing is everything!

Finally, be open to finding a qualified professional counselor to assist you. It is not a sign of weakness to seek guidance and wisdom from those who are trained to help you navigate the challenges of divorce. Resources are listed in the back of this book.

Spiritual Formation: Applying ancient practices to modern-day problems

James Fenhagen, in his book *Invitation to Holiness*, explains, "The Christian life involves more than growth and development. It involves conversion and transformation, a radical turning of the self toward God who made us and who continues to sustain us. Christian faith is about an inner transformation of consciousness resulting from our encounter with the living Christ."[2] This is the process of spiritual formation—conversion and transformation, turning toward God, and an encounter with the living Christ.

If we take as our premise that this life is about soul-making—that is, spiritual formation—then it is possible to see life not as a series of disconnected experiences, but rather as a process by which we can participate with God in the development of our spiritual nature. Note the emphasis is on the process rather than the end result, thus the metaphor of the journey, which implies movement rather than stasis.

The Bible is filled with stories of spiritual journeys; one might even argue that the Bible is the story of humankind's journey toward God. Certainly Jesus' own life is an example of such a journey with each experience linking to the next. Each joy, triumph, pain, and disappointment moves toward the ultimate union (or in Jesus' case, reunion) with God in Christ's resurrection.

What is clearly evident, however, is that while this world is indeed the vale of soul-making, it is also, at times, the vale of tears. Suffering is part and parcel of the journey of life. And yet, despite this fact, suffering is all too often relegated to the back page of the church bulletin in the prayer list. It seems to me that we miss the miracle of redemption in suffering—the way in which God will take what is meant for evil and turn it into good—when we are too focused on the miracle of healing. We forget, or perhaps do not notice, that Jesus did not heal most of the people He met. That He did choose to heal some remains a mystery. Why some and not all?

What is not a mystery is that Jesus can be found in the midst of pain and that suffering can bring us to a richer and deeper faith. But this is a process in which we must participate. God in His unfathomable wisdom has chosen to work with us and through us to complete His good work. Over the centuries, Christians have discovered practices that assist in this endeavor by opening our hearts and minds to the voice of God. Just as Jesus balanced His time of engagement with others with times of separation, these practices assist the believer in moving between action and meditation. Much like the story of Mary and Martha, we struggle to find the balance between work and prayer—between sitting at Jesus' feet and doing the dishes. Both have their place in spiritual expression, and you will find the exercises in this book will include both active and contemplative spiritual practices.

Given the breadth and depth of the topic of spiritual formation and disciplines, I will only touch on some of the most common in this book. I have included some suggested readings at the end of this book if you are interested in exploring this topic further. For our purposes, though, the following practices will be suggested throughout this book.

1. Studying Scripture. This is the most common spiritual practice and one that involves reading Scripture with the goal of determining how to apply its teachings to our lives. For Christians, this discipline assumes the work of the Holy Spirit in assisting us with insight and understanding. Thus, studying Scripture is not just about our efforts to learn but also about God's willingness to teach us.

2. Meditating on Scripture. In addition to study, Scripture can be used as a means for meditation. One example of this is a practice called *lectio divina*—or sacred reading. It is a practice in which a small portion of Scripture, perhaps three or four verses, is read slowly and prayerfully, several times over. The objective is to open up to a conversation with God. This takes places in four stages:

   a. Slowly reading the Scripture passage. Taking time to notice words, images, or phrases that stand out and then spending time in prayer and consideration.

   b. Meditating on the passage. Reflecting on the intent of the Scripture and allowing the words to sink in. Seeking to see what this reveals about ourselves and our relationship to God.

   c. Praying in response to what has been revealed. Speaking to God directly about our needs and the challenges we face. Expressing gratitude for grace and mercy.

    d.   Contemplating the experience. Sitting quietly, wordlessly; letting go and being receptive to God's presence in the moment.

3. Imagining ourselves in Scripture. Using our imagination to "see" ourselves as part of the story we are reading—as the blind man who was healed by Christ, as the rich young king who could not follow Christ, as Mary at the feet of Jesus—can help us to unearth a deeper meaning of stories we may have heard all our lives.

4. Praying. Prayer is multi-faceted since it takes on many forms and shapes depending on the circumstances and the person who is praying. Some prayers are simple cries for help. Others can be responses of acceptance of God's will. Still others are prayers of gratitude and thanksgiving.

    a.   Writing out your prayers. For some, prayer can become more meaningful when it is written. As one writes, words might spring forth that connect to some deeper part of one's own self and reveal desires, wounds, or gratitude that would not be accessible otherwise.

    b.   Breath prayer. A breath prayer is a short prayer that can be said in one inhalation and one exhalation of breath. The most common is called the Jesus Prayer: "Lord Jesus Christ, Son of God, have mercy on me." But you can use a Scripture passage or create your own breath prayer. A breath prayer can be said anytime, anyplace, anywhere to help us to focus our minds on God.

    c.   Praying the Psalms. The Book of Psalms is the prayer book of the Bible. They run the gamut of emotions, from praise and thanksgiving to anger and sorrow. Reading the Psalms prayerfully allows us to bring to God all of our emotions—our hurt, pain, anger, and frustration, as well as joy and gratitude.

    d.   Praying contemplatively. Contemplative prayer can take many forms. One suggested by Thomas Merton is called "centering prayer." To practice this, one selects a meaningful word (Jesus, love, peace, God) and repeats this while clearing one's mind of distracting thoughts or images. Sometimes the use of a candle or other object to gaze at can help to maintain this posture. This is a form of meditation, but unlike some Eastern practices in which the goal is to empty yourself, Christian meditation seeks to fill you with God's love, mercy, and grace.

5. Service to others. The Christian is called to be Christ to the world. While we cannot do this without the empowerment of the Holy Spirit, we must be willing to carry out this mandate in whatever form it may take.

     a. Responding to others as though they were Christ. This is probably the most difficult task we are asked to do, particularly when that person is not very lovable. The above listed spiritual practices can assist us in responding to this call.

     b. Using your gifts to enrich the world. The Bible teaches that we are all gifted in unique ways for God's service. And when we use these gifts, we fulfill not only our calling but ourselves as well.

Relationships as spiritual formation experiences

At the end of each chapter, you will find at least one of these practices included as an activity to assist you in this process of spiritual formation. But spiritual practices, or disciplines as they are also called, are not the only means for spiritual formation. Relationships can serve this function as well. This is the case even—or perhaps most especially—in challenging relationships.

Though you are, or soon will be, divorced from your spouse, you will still be in relationship. Those who have been divorced long enough will attest to this truth. Divorce does not end a relationship; it changes a relationship. And the more emotionally intense the process of divorce was, the more negative emotional baggage we carry with us throughout our life. This can be seen in the way grown children of divorce agonize over seating

arrangements at a wedding. "We can't have Mom sitting next to D
though Mom and Dad may have been divorced for years, the emotional
intensity remains as strong as ever.

You, however, can create a different outcome for yourself. By seeing this
time as an opportunity for personal and spiritual growth, you can sow the
seeds of a peaceful divorce. To accomplish this, you will need to make a
simple yet difficult change in yourself: You will need to learn how to respond
differently to your former spouse. You will learn, for example, how to change
the way you habitually react to your former spouse, which in turn, helps you
in every other relationship. And, more importantly, it will help you to navigate your divorce away from the war zone and into a more livable terrain.

In the chapters that follow, we will build upon these foundational ideas
so that you can use this time to fully grieve the loss of your marriage, to learn
to use this opportunity for personal and emotional growth, and to cooperate
in the process of spiritual formation. In the next chapter, you will encounter
the story of Candace. As you read her story, see if you can identify the ways
in which she grew herself in the process of her divorce.

1. Review the list of spiritual disciplines in this chapter. Which of
these do you find most appealing? Why do you think this is so?
Which do you think will be the most challenging? Why?

2. Read the story of Joseph in Genesis chapters 37–45. Imagine yourself as Joseph in each of the situations in which he found himself.
Ask the Holy Spirit to reveal to you the lesson you most need to
learn right now. Write about what you learn in your journal.

CHAPTER TWO

Awakening
(Candace's Story)

And under the trees, beyond time's brittle drift
I stood like Adam in his lonely garden
On that first morning, shaken out of sleep,
Rubbing his eyes, listening, parting the leaves,
Like tissue on some vast, incredible gift.
—Mary Oliver
New and Selected Poems

Now I feel like Rip Van Winkle, waking up after years and thriving! So much of my life was spent living a pretense; it was as though I was sleepwalking, going through the motions, but not really being in touch with who I was or what I wanted. I was so concerned with living up to other people's expectation, or what I thought their expectations were, that I didn't have a clue as to what I wanted. Growing up, I always felt as though I was a disappointment in some way. I was supposed to have been a boy. My name was to have been Mark. So I knew that even from the beginning, I had disappointed my parents, my father in particular. I always had the feeling I was second best in his eyes.

In addition, my dad was a major perfectionist. If you were to look up the word perfect in the dictionary, there would be a picture of my dad. I hated living up to his expectations, but that was the script in our family. One of our family bylines was "what would the neighbors think," not what would our family think, or feel, but "what would the neighbors think." My mom was an alcoholic; I'd have been an alcoholic, too, if I'd been married to my dad. So there was a lot of pressure to present a certain outward image that at times was very different from the truth.

I met my husband at the end of my junior year in high school, and I believed he was the answer to my every need. We got engaged, and I had sexual intercourse for the first time and I got pregnant the following month. So I was two months pregnant when we got married. Now what would the neighbors think of me! I carried the full shame, guilt, depression, and blame. It never occurred to me to think that he was also to blame! As it turned out, I discovered that I had married a man to whom I was also second best. His first choice was a tall, thin, blond girl whom he had dated in high school. I guess I was more the appropriate type for a minister's wife, which is what he was studying to be, and I guess because I got pregnant, he decided that the right thing to do was to go ahead with the marriage. But throughout our marriage, I always felt that he withheld his approval, affection, and acceptance of me.

Later, when he became the pastor of a church, I struggled to live up to the expectations of a pastor's wife, though sometimes I had my own little ways of rebelling. Sometimes I would purposely not do some of the things the older ladies said I should, just because they said so. But I was lonely. What can I say—I was very lonely.

Outwardly, we looked fine. My husband was not a stingy man, he provided for us, he was a good father, but there was no inner warmth. We called him the "Teflon man" because nothing stuck. In public he was extremely charismatic, funny, a great storyteller, but no one was his intimate friend. Still, I always believed that if I were better, he would be able to love me the way I wanted to be loved. So I worked my butt off. I even had my hair dyed blond, and I kept my weight at my high school weight; I kept searching for the right key. I searched for almost 30 years.

I think a significant turning point in our marriage came on our fifteenth anniversary, when we went to Hawaii. At that time, my husband had left the position of pastor of our church and was working in a different capacity for our denomination. But he told me on the way home that he missed the pulpit and that he was going back to being the minister of our former church. I asked, "You mean you are going to do two full-time jobs?" He just said, "Everything will work out." My heart sank. I'd always felt I was second, but now I was going to be third-best in his life. I remember thinking to myself, *I will find somebody to love me.* I seemed to realize that what I wanted to have from my husband—the kind of attention and emotional intimacy that I had always longed for—would never happen. I think that was the beginning of the end for my marriage.

Within five years, I found myself powerfully attracted to another man, and we had an affair. I became a person I did not like—a liar, a sneak, a cheat. I had lived my entire life trying to be perfect, and I had such guilt over becoming pregnant out of wedlock. I couldn't believe that I had committed adultery. But my need to be loved was bigger than my fear of God. Even so, I was aware that this relationship was a dead end from the beginning, and when he pressed me to get a divorce, I knew I couldn't do it. I remember crying out to God, "I want to do it Your way, even though a part of me doesn't want to." I surrendered and ended the relationship with this other man.

Later, my husband and I took a short trip up the coast and he asked me, "Have you ever been unfaithful?" I did not lie; I did not skirt the issue. That was the day the marriage ended for him. It took him ten years to leave because it was very necessary for him to be the offended person and to be the one who did the right thing. So he stayed until our youngest child went to college. It was 10 years of hell.

During that time, I went into counseling and I began to understand that I was only responsible for my part of our marital difficulties. I also learned that I could allow God to bring me into a position of loving my husband, respecting him and opening myself up to him. And it happened; at least it happened for me. Sometimes, though, I was angry because it seemed like I was the only one doing any work on our marriage. I'd ask him, "Why can't you just forgive me?" And he'd say, "I have forgiven you." But then he'd keep bringing up the affair.

Of course, my husband was very supportive about my being in counseling because in his opinion, I needed to be fixed. He would attend, too, but not for more than three sessions, because he could see at that point that the counselor was looking to try to work with him and he didn't want that, so he quit. But I continued to go to counseling on my own in order to survive and, I suppose, to keep my marriage. My greatest fear was that he would leave me and I would be abandoned. I continued to hope that if I found the right key, our lives would be different.

The day he left, after our son left for college, was the day I finally gave up hope. I came home from work that day, knowing that he was moving out, still hoping that when I got home he would just have taken a few of his things. He took everything that was his! Everything! I was completely devastated. I realized that my greatest fear had come true.

I fell on the floor in my bedroom, and I just rolled back and forth. I was overcome with terror at being alone. I had always known what it was like to be lonely, but I had never been alone. But as I lay there, crying, I felt God speaking to me, and saying that He would never leave me, and I would never be alone. And that was a major life-changing event for me. Major.

I settled down and a peace came over me. I continued to lie on the floor for about half an hour until some friends called and said they were coming to get me and take me to dinner. And that was the day I had to grow up and grow up quickly. I was really alone; it was fact, not a fear. Though I still hate divorce, I probably would never have grown without first being alone. I think the steps toward my healing started then.

My counselor directed me to the Overcomers program, a Christian 12-step program. Her concern was that I not stay in the house and be isolated and also that I would have an opportunity to struggle with my codependency issues in a context of safety. I guess my motto at that time was "instead of being perfect, I'd rather be real." And this group turned out to be the best thing for me. Even though I was feeling sad, angry, and lonely at that time, for the first time in my life, I forgave myself for not being perfect. As a result, I became open to people, and I found that I am not so much different from anybody else.

The first year or so was very difficult because I was in the house—our family home—alone. So I learned a lot of things very quickly. For instance, one of the things I had wanted to do, but had not been allowed to do, was listen to Christian music. My husband didn't want to listen to that kind of music after being at church all day. So during this time, I immersed myself in Christian music during the day and sometimes even in the middle of the night. You know, when you're going through a time of grief, the nights can be horribly, horribly long. So during this time I'd wake up at night, often with a panic attack, and I'd turn the TV on to this program that played Christian music against a backdrop of beautiful photographs. I'd watch that and get myself into a peaceful state, and then I'd wake up again, often around 4:30 or 5:00 a.m., and put on my shoes and go walking.

In addition to my counselor and the Overcomers group, I relied on my friendships. I had three intimate friends, two female and one male, and they just let me say whatever I needed to say. They never put any kind of guilt trip on me or judged me, and that was really invaluable. I made some new friends, too. I told a friend of mine early on, "I am going to surround myself with winners." I've seen divorce destroy too many people, and I didn't want to be one of those. So that's what I did. I consciously decided to spend time with people who were making a positive impact with their lives. In fact, there were some people I wouldn't associate with because they were so negative. If they called, I decided not to return their calls. I had too much to deal with without having anybody encourage my negativity.

One thing I learned that was really vital for my recovery was to have something to look forward to. I would never let a holiday sneak up on me without any plans. I determined all holidays would be done differently; I would not try to replicate the family traditions.

The weekends were the toughest for me. Monday through Thursday was fine, but I hated those weekend nights. So I learned to take the initiative and make plans. I found out that if I didn't make sure I had plans, then I was in trouble. I learned that I could be the entertainment chairman of my life—that I didn't have to rely on my husband for that. I found out I could choose who I would be with and I could go to the places I wanted to go, and see the movies I wanted to see. I always made sure I had something planned at least six or eight weeks ahead that I could look forward to, whether it was a three-day weekend up to Oxnard to see my friends, or a trip to see my family in Arkansas.

Throughout this time, I continued to work full-time, and even though I often didn't feel like it, I made it a point to be better dressed than I had ever dressed and have my makeup just right. I wasn't trying to be perfect, but took care of myself in a way that showed I could still be a professional and deal with my personal issues when I got home.

My goal at that point was to live a balanced life. I had been out of balance for so long and I didn't know what a balanced life looked like. I decided to go back to school. I felt like I was doing everything I could for the emotional part of me, so I needed to address the intellectual part, too. I took a class in early American history, an art class, and a horticulture class. It was great. I also began to attend a new church, which helped me with the spiritual aspect of my life.

Perhaps the most meaningful change for me during this time was that I reconnected with my sisters. The week after my husband moved out, my sisters sent me a box of Jonathan apples. They knew that Jonathan apples are my favorites and that they are in season for only a short time. To this day I am moved by this memory because their gesture was so tender. It broke every barrier I had put up. Plus, I think that because I was no longer putting up a perfect front, I wanted to get to know them, too.

During this time, I kept two notes in my wallet that I could refer to as many times as I wanted to. One said "Stay in Today," and the other, from my counselor, said "Time plus Truth plus Grace equals Healing." I knew nothing of grace and no one knew the truth about me, but I was finding out about both of these in my journey. My sisters' gift was an example of grace.

My house finally sold, and my friends and I took a whole day to hunt for an apartment. I knew exactly what I had in mind. I wanted something practically new, very clean, within my budget, and with an ocean view. After almost purchasing a condo, and deciding to wait, I drove up to this place that just happened to have an apartment come available, and it had an ocean view from the patio. It was a glorious place! I could hardly wait to get home every day so I could watch the sun go down and just heal. That's when I began to discover, or I began to allow, the creative side of me to come out.

The interesting thing is that we still weren't legally divorced. My husband wanted me to divorce him since I had been the one who had committed adultery. I said to him, "You know what, big boy? I have taken the blame for you for the last time. If you want a divorce, go get it!" When he saw that I meant what I said, he finally did. Now this was new behavior for me. Boundaries have never been my thing. And it felt good because I didn't do it in anger. It was one of the first times I had spoken to him and set a boundary without it being an angry boundary. I was very firm.

Shortly after that, my son was planning to get married. His dad, who was no longer in the ministry, was going to perform the ceremony at the church where we had been a family, so it was really very, very difficult. In addition, the family my son was marrying into did not have very kind feelings toward me, so I knew it was going to be a big challenge.

My girlfriends and I took a trip up to Santa Barbara to buy my dress for the wedding. It was stunning, absolutely stunning! In addition, my son was getting married on my birthday, and in some ways, I felt like the wedding reception was my coming-out party, in spite of all the grief the bride's family gave me. For instance, they had ordered limos to go from the church to the reception, but they didn't invite me to ride in one although they had invited people who were not even family members. So I just invited myself right in and said, "Scoot down; I need a little more room!" I felt really empowered.

Later, as we walked into the hotel, my ex-husband kept walking three steps ahead of me. I just picked up my dress and put my arm through his.

"I need somebody to walk me in," I said. "And since you're the Dad and I'm the Mom, it's you!" To this day, he can't stand to be around me. I make him nervous, very nervous!

Somewhere in this process, before the divorce was final, the lady who had sold my home called me. I remember thinking, *Why are you calling me? You've got your money!* She asked if I was dating, and I said, "Of course not! Why did you ask?" She explained that she knew this nice man who was "some kind of Christian" and that if I needed an escort or someone to go to coffee with, she thought we would just really enjoy each other. I told her I'd call her back in about six months because I couldn't even think about that then. And six months later, my friend Steve called and said, "It's time."

I met Bob, the man my realtor had mentioned, and I really enjoyed his company. We just clicked right away. One time I said to him, "Why is a man like you still single?" and he said, "Well, I guess it's just taken God this much time to get me ready for you." We've cried together. We both wish we had never been divorced.

He said to me once, "What we have done, and what we have learned, even though it's been a hard, hard lesson—and it's sad—has made us who we are today. Let's make the most of what we have." He is that kind of a special man. He is a gift.

So now my motto is, "Living well is the best revenge." I plan to be happy and enjoy something about each and every day I have on this earth. I'm still not blond; I'm heavier than I have ever been in my life, but I love my life. I learned a new word recently, "praxis." I nearly shouted "hallelujah" when I heard this word. It means "the integration of belief with behavior." I never had that in my life. I had guilt. I had perfectionism. So my belief system was not integrated with my behavior. To me, the part that grace plays in your life is so you can have praxis in your life. Today, I like me. I like my spontaneity, generosity, compassion, laughter, humor. I am learning to forgive others, to set realistic expectations for myself, and to see that I am a work in progress.

The neat thing is that people feel more comfortable around me now, too. I've become more relaxed. One person at work told me just last week,

"Oh, I like you so much better now!" I became approachable when I didn't have to work so hard at trying to be perfect. I also worked through a lot of anger I had held onto from even before my marriage. Once I got through that, it was like I had more room for something else in my life.

Probably the greatest thing that has happened is that my kids are responding differently to me now, too. I think that over the years since my divorce they have seen me behave with consistency; they can see that I am being who I really am. I'm very upfront. And even though initially they held back, I think now they are moving into a different kind of relationship with me. My son gave me the most incredible gift this Mother's Day. He and his wife had put together a memory album entitled, "The Story of Mom and Me." He had the photos that I had given him from his growing-up years and wrote a little comment by each one of them. It was just the nicest, nicest tribute to have that from him. I'll never be the same again.

When I look back at where I have come from, and the person I used to be, it still amazes me. That's all I can say. It still amazes me. And now I can truly say, "I don't want to go back." I look forward to what God wants me to do. I am truly learning to stay in today. I used to be trapped in the guilt of the past and the fear of the future, and I lost out on today. Well, I don't plan to miss out anymore!

REFLECTION

"What is REAL?" asked the Rabbit one day, when they were lying side by side near the nursery fender, before Nana came to tidy the room. "Does it mean having things that buzz inside you and a stick-out handle?"

"Real isn't how you are made," said the Skin Horse. "It's a thing that happens to you. When a child loves you for a long, long time, not just to play with, but really loves you, then you become Real."

"Does it hurt?" asked the Rabbit.

"Sometimes," said the Skin Horse, for he was always truthful. "When you are Real, you don't mind being hurt."

"Does it happen all at once, like being wound up," he asked, "or bit by bit?"

"It doesn't happen all at once," said the Skin Horse. "You become. It takes a long time. That's why it doesn't often happen to people who break easily, or have sharp edges, or who have to be carefully kept."

—MARGERY WILLIAMS
The Velveteen Rabbit

What the Velveteen Rabbit learned, and what Candace's story teaches us, is that beauty and wisdom come from an inner source, not from an outward representation. When Candace says that her motto became, "Instead of being perfect, I'd rather be real," she encapsulates the essence of this story, as well as the wisdom that her journey through loss and grief has brought her. Becoming real is a painful process, particularly when we have clung so tenaciously to the belief that in order to be loved, we must be perfect. And yet, as Candace learned, and as all those who have shared in her experience and been willing to give up the quest for perfection have discovered, we can never be truly loved until we are willing to be real.

And this is the inherent irony in the quest for perfection. It is only in giving up the quest that we find the love that was its aim. Jungian analyst Marion Woodman discusses this in her work, *Addiction to Perfection*.[1] The quest for perfection is one that ultimately leads to death. In a very real sense, perfectionism assumes that one can become like God. But it is not given to human beings to be perfect. Rather we are to strive toward wholeness, which means acknowledging and honoring all aspects of ourselves. We need to acknowledge the void from which we are fleeing in our quest for perfection. In addition, we need to ground ourselves in the feminine side of God, in the positive nourishing aspect. When this happens, we can surrender. We can let life happen. We can allow life to pour through us.

This surrender can be seen in Candace's story as she lay on the floor in her bedroom the day her husband left. She felt the terror of the void, which lies at the heart of the fear of abandonment. And somehow, in that moment of surrender, she encountered the still small voice of God. "I will never leave," were the words Candace heard spoken. And thus began her journey toward wholeness.

From that point onward, evidence of a newfound ability to self-nurture can be seen throughout Candace's story. She continues in her personal therapy; she begins to attend a support group. She seeks, and finds, a physical place that would feel nurturing and healing. Her home becomes her refuge. And as she allows this nurturing aspect to become activated, she discovers a newfound creativity.

Creativity is a sign of life, as well as a characteristic of God. In her surrender, Candace was able to allow God to be manifested in her life. One associates creativity with spring. The end of a long winter is heralded by the new bright green buds that emerge through the snow. And so, for Candace, the winter of her grief prepared the way for new life to emerge.

This is the hallmark of transformation. Candace did not merely survive her grief; she was transformed by it. It is telling that her colleague notes the change in her by remarking, "Oh, I like you so much better now!" Candace herself is aware of the tremendous change within her. Feeling like Rip Van Winkle, awakening to a new world, is her metaphor for her experience. Again, this movement from being asleep, or unconscious, toward consciousness is an outgrowth of transformation.

But there can be a price paid for consciousness. Life is no longer so simple; it ceases to be characterized by black and white and emerges colored by shades of gray. Furthermore, consciousness often begets authenticity. And when one begins to act out of an authentic, thoughtful predetermination, one can never return to the unconscious identification with any one group or ideology.

1. Perfectionism is sometimes wrongly equated with striving toward excellence. But as you have seen in this story, perfectionism can keep us from experiencing joy in our relationship with God and others. Make an honest inventory of your life and evaluate where

perfectionism may be getting in your way. Perhaps you tell yourself you must be the perfect parent, or perhaps you avoid revealing struggles that you are having to others in an effort to keep up a façade. Take a moment to identify a relationship in which your perfectionism is keeping you from being real and authentic. What might you do to begin to change that?

2. Read Genesis 3. How might perfectionism be related to the desire to "be like God"? How did this desire affect Adam and Eve's relationship with God?

3. Centering prayer. Take five or ten minutes today and practice centering prayer. Select a word or phrase from Scripture that is particularly meaningful to you. As you repeat this word or phrase, allow the unrelated thoughts that come into your mind to drift away. You will find this difficult at first since it is so easy to be caught up in the day-to-day worries and concerns of our lives. But continue to sit quietly and allow the Holy Spirit to minister to you.

CHAPTER THREE

The Importance of Grief

I was completely devastated. I realized that my greatest fear had come true. I fell on the floor in my bedroom, and I just rolled back and forth. I was overcome with the terror of being alone.

—Candace

Not finding satisfaction in anything or understanding anything in particular, and remaining in its emptiness and darkness, it [the soul] embraces all things with great preparedness.

—St. John of the Cross

When it comes to divorce, grief is the last emotion that comes to mind; instead, anger, bitterness, and betrayal all clamor for the spotlight. As a result, grief is relegated to the sidelines and given little, if any, recognition by anyone, including—and perhaps most especially—the people involved.

In some ways this is understandable. Grief is a terrifying emotion. This is what C.S. Lewis discovered after the death of his wife, Joy Davidman: "No one ever told me that grief is so like fear. I am not afraid, but the sensation is like being afraid."[1] Alan Paton, author of *Cry, the Beloved Country*, describes his grief as emptiness: "It is the empty house that shouts at me, the empty desolate silent house, the house where you are not, the house where you would be waiting for me to return from one journey or other."[2]

But these searingly honest depictions of grief are rare in our society. When was the last time you heard someone really speak honestly about grief and loss? Or, perhaps more to the point, when have you felt comfortable expressing your grief and sadness? If you are like most people, you felt constrained and inhibited from revealing the truth of your pain, even to those closest to you. This is because as a society, we are held in the grip of a pervasive attitude that discounts the experience of suffering and advocates a quick fix, get-over-it approach, particularly when it comes to grief in divorce.

Recently a client of mine sat crying softly in my office, trying to come to terms with her divorce after twenty-six-years of marriage. "I don't know why I'm crying," she said, "other people have it so much worse!" I can't imagine that a widow would say that. Yet my client's response is very typical of those who are going through a divorce. "I don't know why I'm crying!" reveals a tremendous disconnect between the grief in her heart and the idea in her head that divorce doesn't merit grief. What is it about divorce that makes it so difficult to recognize, let alone honor, the grief that it brings?

This cultural blind spot is partly a result of our attitudes toward grief in general. As British sociologist Geoffrey Gorer observes, "Mourning is treated as if it were a weakness, a self-indulgence, a reprehensible bad habit instead of as a psychological necessity."[3] In an effort to try to avoid the pain of grief, we have abandoned the rituals that once brought comfort to those left behind: a fixed period of mourning, black armbands, dark clothing, formal rituals.

From the early days of my widowhood I remember wishing for some sort of outward sign that I was in mourning: the old-fashioned tradition of wearing black, a sign that communicated "handle with care." Instead, I was faced with the task of navigating in secret the strange and foreign territory that was now my life. Short of announcing to everyone I met that I had just lost my husband, there was no way to signal the woundedness of my inward condition, no societal recognition of an experience that our ancestors understood for what it is—a life-changing, post-Katrina event, the kind that leaves a wasteland where there once was life and warmth.

Our modern response to grief is to make it a personal rather than a communal event, which creates a tacit agreement to keep grief in the closet. "Don't ask; don't tell" seems to be the byword. Don't ask about someone else's suffering and don't tell others about yours. This attitude is, in turn, a reflection of our aversion to suffering of any kind. At the first sign of pain, we quickly run to the nearest form of relief: medication, alcohol, work, relationships, or thrill seeking. Without really knowing it, we hold deeply the expectation that life should be smooth and easy, that we should not have to face pain and suffering. The irony is that when we do encounter times of pain, we feel impressed to hide it as a shameful secret from others and from ourselves.

If our efforts to eradicate pain were successful we would expect that people would be living happier more fulfilling lives. Instead, what we find is that emotional disorders such as depression and anxiety are on the rise. The less suffering we have had to endure, the less able we are to tolerate the suffering that does manage to confront us. And yet, it is our denial of the mysterious quality of pain that keeps us from learning the lessons it has to teach.

I have witnessed this time and again in my work as a psychologist. Clients have come to see me after years of medical management for depression that has resulted in countless permutations of anti-depressants, anti-anxiety medications, and mood stabilizers. By the time I see them, they are rightly demoralized and discouraged. When I suggest that we begin to listen to their pain and suffering and discover what it has to tell us, it comes as both a relief and a surprise.

Our cultural denial of pain—particularly emotional pain—affects our response to grief. Grief has become a pathological condition that now requires a host of experts to address. Rather than simply experiencing grief and its concomitant pain and suffering, we are given checklists for moving through the stages of grief that are aimed at achieving some kind of "closure." Grief is something to recover from, so we now have grief recovery programs, support groups, and specialists. To add insult to injury, grief that goes on "too long" is also often categorized as a mental disorder.

In the eyes of many people—professionals as well as the average individual—grief and depression are inextricably linked. The same medications prescribed for depression are recommended for those who have been bereaved. I'll never forget the conversation I had with a neighbor a few months after her husband of almost fifty years died of a heart attack. She had just returned from a visit to her family doctor who had given her a prescription for anti-depressants. I knew she wasn't depressed; in fact, I was impressed with the way in which she was handling her loss. Her physician, on the other hand, responded to her normal grief as though it were an illness. This is a testament to the price we all pay for our collusion in the denial of pain.

The siren call of a pain-free existence is so entrancing that it takes a tremendous act of will to resist it. Our current attitudes rob pain of its potential for meaning, and meaningless suffering is the worst kind of suffering. But let's consider the possibility that pain can have meaning, that suffering does have some lessons to teach. If this is true, then we are only robbing ourselves of the opportunities that times of trial present to us, and in the long run we end up creating more suffering.

As I often say to my clients who are in the throes of divorce: "If you have to go through suffering, let's make it count for something. Let's learn from it."

British psychologist John Bowlby, in his study of infants who were placed in an orphanage, observed the most raw and painful expressions of grief. He noted that the loss of a loved one is "one of the most intensely painful experiences any human being can suffer."[4] This aspect of grief is part of what makes it so challenging for those who are divorcing. The body responds to grief as if the former spouse were dead, but the mind knows he or she is not. It is difficult to let go of someone who has died to you (your former spouse) and yet remains on this earth. Just when you think you have let go a bit, the one whose loss you are grieving is standing on your doorstep or leaving a message on your phone.

This creates the ambivalence so many people experience as they go through divorce. It is seen in the second-guessing that often occurs by those who may have initiated the divorce. It is evident in the last-ditch efforts to reunite and the brief honeymoon period that quickly devolves into one more round of fighting and acrimony. "Why am I missing him so much?!" one of my clients used to tearfully exclaim. "I know I don't want to go back to all the pain and fighting. But my heart still thinks that maybe he'll be different."

Phases of grief in divorce

The bonds we create when we are married are not so easily broken. Learning to learn to identify the somewhat unique aspects of grief after divorce will help you to more effectively navigate the emotional and spiritual challenges. Though these characteristics will intersect and often reoccur throughout the grief process, they tend to be clustered into six phases: Refusal, Negotiation, Upheaval, Acceptance, Emergence and Launching.

Phase One: Refusal

In the first phase of divorce, Refusal, the individual struggles to take in the fact of divorce on an emotional level. This is, in part, the result of our inborn reaction to deep emotional pain. "This can't be happening to me," is a common thought during this time. "I was stunned," writes Gillis describing her reaction to her husband's announcement that he wanted a divorce. "I didn't know what to say, what to do, so I said nothing, showed nothing. I searched my feelings—I didn't seem to have any: no pain, no emotion, nothing." It is an experience that psychologists call "de-realization" in which the world seems unreal.

For some people, this phase is more subtle. A vague awareness may slowly crystallize into focus after years of efforts to change, accommodate, hope, pray and, at times, deny until finally the realization hits home: "This marriage is not going to work." For these individuals, the refusal stage lasts a very long time.

This was the case for Pamela. During her difficult 18-year marriage, she heard her husband consistently assert: "I'm not the problem; you're the problem." For most of her marriage, she tried to accommodate his ever-shifting demands, but eventually she realized that nothing she did was good enough.

When she came to me, she was on an emotional roller coaster, vacillating between begging him to acknowledge her efforts and screaming at him for being so impossible to live with. Though we did not know it at the time, Pamela was in the refusal stage of divorce. She was beginning to accept that despite all her efforts, she could never have the marriage she dreamed of with her husband.

She decided to stop "twisting herself into a pretzel," as she put it, in order to please her husband and instead allowed her values to guide her behavior. Though this was a positive step for Pamela, it soon became apparent that her husband preferred their former style of marriage and he decided to file for divorce. Pamela was initially devastated by his decision but quickly regained her equilibrium. "In my heart I knew our marriage had been dying for a long time," she recalled. "I just hadn't been willing to accept it."

Phase Two: Negotiation

The next phase, Negotiation, is seen in the bargaining that occurs with one's spouse—and with God—to avoid the inevitable. As Candace described her negotiation in the Refusal phase, "I continued to hope that if I found the right key, our lives would be different." Finding the "right key" is the theme of this phase of divorce—the belief that you just need to say or do the right thing to unlock the door to prevent the divorce. It is evidenced by the last-ditch efforts to make things work, the sporadic attempts to reunite, the phone call to the counselor before the one made to the attorney. It is the final "No!" before the quiet "yes" of begrudging acceptance.

Like the Refusal phase, Negotiation can last a long time. John, a 50-year-old father of two, had been in this stage for about ten years when he came to see me. His wife had been unhappy with him for much of their marriage.

He focused a considerable amount of his energy on trying to keep her from being upset, which, ironically, only made things worse. He believed that he needed to find the magic formula—the script of behaviors and responses— that would make her happy.

He ended up being so anxious that he was unable to be relaxed and comfortable around her. And yet, despite the fact that both he and his wife were miserable in their marriage, it was very difficult for John to see how his efforts to make his wife happy were only contributing to their difficulties. Change was too frightening for him. Once his wife decided to separate, he was surprised to find that he felt relieved.

Phase Three: Upheaval

In the next phase of divorce, Upheaval, life is not as it once was and yet it is not what is to come. Abigail Trafford calls this "Crazy Time," in her book of the same name. "There seems to be no end to this wild swinging back and forth. You can't believe how bad your life is, how terrible you feel, how overwhelming daily tasks become, how frightened you are: about money, your health, your sanity."[5] It is difficult for us to navigate through this time of the unknown, when all the rules have been broken and nothing seems to make sense.

It is during the Upheaval phase that the truth of what has happened finally sinks in. "Now I am really on my own" is the thought that characterizes this phase, and it is in many ways the most painful to endure. This is the time when people are most likely to seek out a new relationship just to ease the pain. But these relationships usually compound the pain in the long run—and prolong the grief experience. Most importantly, running into the arms of another stops the transformative process and denies you the opportunity to create the new life that you have yet to imagine.

The Upheaval stage was particularly challenging for Marcia, who came to see me after countless attempts to save her twenty-five-year marriage. During this phase, Marcia was plagued with fears and doubts. She and her husband would reunite for brief periods and then she would realize, "I can't be married to this man for the rest of my life. I can't love him the way he needs to be loved, and he can't love me in the way I need to be loved either."

Once they were separated for a while, she would worry that she was making a big mistake and might regret her decision to leave the marriage. Despite all the confusion and disequilibrium, Marcia resisted the urge to file for divorce before she was really ready and focused instead on learning what she could about herself and her contribution to the challenges in her marriage. "I don't want to repeat the last twenty-five years with anyone else," she explained. "Next time, I want to do things differently. I want to learn to stop hiding out in my marriage and instead really be myself."

Phase Four: Acceptance

From the stormy seas of the Upheaval phase, Acceptance, the quieter phase of grief, will gradually emerge—usually in fits and starts. Moments of acceptance are followed by days of upheaval, until the times of acceptance become longer and the crazy time dies down. One client described her first experience of acceptance this way: "I was sitting in the living room after the kids had gone to sleep, and I realized how quiet and peaceful everything was. I finally had the sanctuary I had been trying to create all my married life but never could. I wasn't worried about him anymore—when was he going to come home and why didn't he spend more time with me and the children. I wasn't caught up in the fights and arguments. I felt safe for the first time. I knew in my heart of hearts that we will be okay." Acceptance can't be forced and it can't be hurried. It is the phase everyone would like to get to as quickly as possible, but just as in the experience of giving birth, or reaping a harvest, the timing is not in our direct control.

Phase Five: Emergence

Acceptance naturally flows into the next phase, Emergence. Ancient alchemists called this the "albedo"—the soft moonlit phase of transformation when things can be perceived but dimly as in the shadowy figures visible on a moonlit night. Emergence is the phase of grief in divorce that holds the clear promise of new things to come.

The key characteristic of the Emergence phase is the willingness to finally face some challenge or task that had been unacknowledged or unrecognized during the marriage. This usually means developing something that has lain dormant for many years, maybe even a lifetime. It might be an attitude towards oneself; it might be heeding a call that has been pushed aside by other seemingly more pressing needs; it might be a characteristic that has been undeveloped or a skill or talent that has been hidden away. One thing that is certain: Whatever this task is, it will be unique to each individual and will require courage.

This was certainly the case for Julia, who came to see me after her divorce. As an executive for a large corporation, Julia enjoyed her work but felt emotionally drained and exhausted. Her former husband, a freelance artist, had never contributed much to the family financially, nor did he actively participate in parenting their two children.

During the Emergence phase, Julia became aware of her tendency to placate others by doing the lion's share of the work, not only at home, but at the office as well. Her decision to cut back on her workload and responsibilities was a difficult one as she faced long-held fears and gradually let go of old attitudes. "I'm realizing how easily I give up who I am—what's truly best for me in a situation," she related. "I'm so afraid that others won't like me or that they'll think badly of me that I agree to do things I really don't want to do." Having faced many other challenges in the phases leading up to this one, she was able to build on her prior successes and move forward to the phase of transformation.

Final Phase: Transformation

The final phase of grief in divorce, Transformation, is one in which a person finally has a new experience of life. Something within has changed fundamentally; new knowledge of oneself and the world has resulted in a different response to life. As Maureen described this phase: "I'm much more accepting of myself, which makes me less judgmental of others. I've already broken through the perfection mold with my divorce. I don't run around trying to polish my image all the time. People are going to believe things about me that they want to believe, and though it's still pretty hurtful at times, I realize that, for the most part, it's out of my control.... I have a lot to be grateful for, and I focus on that. It's helped me to learn to let go, and letting go of my ex-husband has helped me to start to let go of my kids in appropriate ways. And that's where I need to be. I'm entering into a new phase of my life because my youngest will be going off to college. So that will be another challenge for me. I'm sure that I'll be moving forward in one way or another in my personal and spiritual growth."

The transformative potential of grief

"Grief is a time when we are blessed with the opportunity to complete a natural process of spiritual death and rebirth before our own death," writes Stephanie Ericsson after the untimely death of her husband in an automobile accident. We go through the dying process while we are still alive, she explains, and experience a spiritual death. We die to self, and it is a frightening experience. And in the end, we find a greater capacity for love and relatedness.[6] These words are echoed by Lynn Caine as she describes herself at the end of her bereavement: "I am another woman now, and I like this woman better. But it was a hard birth."[7]

This idea of "dying to self" is one that is a central focus of Christianity. Jesus spoke of this experience many times, explaining how we need to be ready to give up our own lives in order to follow Him. All too often, this has been simplistically understood as a negation of self, when in truth, it is a fulfillment. The psychologist Carl Jung explained this idea in psychological terms as the need for the ego, or conscious self, to be willing to submit to the call of the larger Self, or the Divine. Our egos are limited in understanding, even of our own selves. "Why do I do that which I don't want to do?" was the question St. Paul asked, and one we all wrestle with. We are a mystery to ourselves.

The transformative potential of grief makes it an act of creativity—as in bringing something new into being. According to the existential psychologist, Rollo May, creativity involves an encounter with the unconscious.[8] The conscious self is confronted with the destruction of previously held notions and attitudes, and it is this destructive aspect of creativity that can be so challenging and painful. Yet it is an essential component of creativity because before something new can come to life, something old must die. As Jesus explained, a seed must die in order for a plant to be born.

Grief thrusts us into this mystery with full force, wresting from us deeply held, but erroneous, assumptions that have hindered us in our personal and spiritual lives. Ideas, such as "I must be perfect in order to be loved and accepted," keep us from experiencing the truth of God's love, mercy, and grace. It is as though in our development as individuals, we put blinders on, resisting the urge to view things from different perspectives out of fear. It is comforting to think you have it all figured out, and at the same time it prevents you from having a vital relationship with God.

So many of the people I interviewed for this book spoke of the implicit pact with God they had made when they got married, such as "If I am a_____ (good Christian, a good wife/husband, a decent human being), then I will have a good marriage." Their divorce called into question this belief and brought home the difficult truth that bad things do happen to good people. And, much like a line of falling dominoes, other beliefs were shattered, too.

In short, the destructive aspect of grief in divorce—while necessary for transformation—is a painful and disorienting experience. For awhile you will stumble around, blindly, like Saul of Tarsus after he saw Christ in a vision. Gradually his sight returned and he entered into the life God had been urging him toward. Paul emerged as a radically changed man. His old system of beliefs had been shattered and now he was ready to be used by God to change the world.

In order to gain from the suffering of grief, you must first accept and recognize that grief in divorce is inevitable. Though the timing may be different for each individual, the challenges of grief confront every divorcing person. But the reward for a grief well-traveled is a more fulfilling and creative life and a deeper and richer relationship with God. This was certainly the experience of Karen, whose story you will read next. See if you can identify some of the ideas covered in this chapter on grief.

1. A theme in this chapter has been to allow yourself to experience your grief in whatever phase you may be. Identifying that phase will assist you not only to understand your experience but also to anticipate the next phase of your life. Review the phases listed below and determine which best describes your life at this moment. Take some time to write in your journal and answer the following questions:

   a. As I allow myself to really experience my life right now, what are my thoughts?

   b. What are the feelings that come with these thoughts? Where do I feel these in my body?

   c. With these thoughts, feelings, and sensations in mind, what do I need to do for myself right now? What would I tell my child or a good friend if they were in this situation? What stops me from saying this to myself?

2. Phases of grief in divorce:

   • Refusal – "This can't be happening to me!"

   • Negotiation – "If only I can find the right key!"

   • Upheaval – "I don't know what to do!"

- Acceptance – "My marriage is over, and I will be alright."

- Emergence – "I'm willing to take a risk and try something new."

- Transformation – "I can't believe I'm the same person I was before my divorce!"

3. Read the story of Christ's crucifixion, death and resurrection in Matthew 26 through 28. Follow this by reading Acts 2. Identify how the phases of grief listed above can be seen in the disciples.

4. In your journal, write a prayer. Allow yourself to write whatever comes to mind; avoid censoring your thoughts and feelings. Keep in mind the Psalms are an example of heartfelt prayers that express every kind of emotion. Read one of the Psalms as an example of how to pray with honesty. As Kathleen Norris explains, "The wide range of expression in the Psalter—the anger and pain of lament, the anguished self-probing of confession, the grateful fervor of thanksgiving, the ecstatic joy of praise—allows us to bring our whole lives before God."[9]

CHAPTER FOUR

Becoming Myself (Karen's Story)

Somehow myself survived the night
And entered with the Day...
—Emily Dickinson

When my husband told me he wanted a divorce, I was totally floored. I felt that my whole world had crashed. We were married for seventeen years, and the divorce hit me from out of the blue. I knew my husband was unhappy, but I had attributed it to the fact that he had suffered a series of losses, including the sudden death of his father, the needs of his mother (who often called him several times a day), and financial setbacks in his business. I tried to get him to go talk to someone, to go to a therapist or a pastor from our church, but he wouldn't.

There were a lot of red flags going up during this time, but when I would mention my concerns to him, he'd just turn it back on me. One major red flag occurred when we went on a family trip to Hawaii. It was supposed to be for ten days, but he left after only a few days, saying he had business that he needed to take care of. It was really odd because that had never happened before. We got into a big fight on the beach because I was questioning him, and he said to me, "If you keep this up, we're going to end up in a divorce." This was the first time I'd ever heard him use the word divorce. So he left and I stayed.

Later, he wanted to go on a trip by himself, but he wouldn't tell me where he was going. He didn't even want me to call him on the phone, but I called him every night on the cell phone. I don't know for sure, but I think he went with another woman because he was staying at bed and breakfasts, which is not something a guy usually does by himself. To this day he swears he didn't, but I guess that's a moot point.

When he returned, he told me he wanted to go to counseling and I said, "Great!" He went to the counselor about three times and after the third session, he came home and said, "The counselor thinks I should tell you something. I want a divorce." I was totally floored. It was so weird. I mean, before he left for his trip, he had sent me a bouquet of roses that was so beautiful I actually took a picture of it. So I was really stunned and confused; I just fell apart. I said to him, "You know, you owe it to me to try marital counseling."

We interviewed three counselors and I let him choose which one for us to go to. He probably went three or four times. At the beginning, he had this list of all the things I had done wrong, basically blaming me for everything. The counselor advised me to let him do his venting with the hope that he might stay in counseling, but he just quit going.

This was an incredibly hard time for me. I was teaching kindergarten, and this whole thing started right before I went back to school. So I really struggled once I returned to the classroom. I would start crying and my teaching partner would have to take over. Finally, the principal asked, "What's going on?" Up to that point I hadn't told anyone about our marital struggles because I kept hoping he would change his mind. But I told the principal, and they cut me some slack at work.

The next three months were incredibly difficult. One day my husband would say he wanted a divorce and the next day he'd say he didn't know. And I was clinging to this hope. I tried to be nicer—to be a good wife. I kept thinking if he just hears the right sermon or if I could say the right thing, maybe he would change his mind.

Finally, about two days before Christmas, he told me he was leaving the day after. So Christmas to me was a total farce. It was horrible. Two days after Christmas, he wanted me to tell the kids that we had decided to get a divorce—that we had grown apart. I said "No." A neighbor of mine had been through a divorce, and he went along with it. To this day, his kids think he wanted it too.

So when my husband started out by saying, "Your mom and I have agreed that we've grown apart...," I said, "No. You have decided that you want a divorce." I had tried to think ahead and figure out what my kids' reaction would be, but I didn't know how bad it would be.

My twelve-year-old said, "I hate you, Dad!" ran upstairs, and slammed the door. My eight-year-old got on his lap and shook him for something like twenty minutes, saying, "You can't do this to me. The whole world is married. Take it back! Take it back! Take it back!"

So he said, "Okay, I'll think about it. Maybe I'll change my mind." Well, I just went ballistic and said, "No. You just tell her now; don't give her hope." And he said, "Well, I might change my mind." Then my daughter came running up to me and said, "See, he might change his mind." But I knew the truth, and after he left, I tried to tell her. And then he went ahead and filed.

I guess that's when I started to pick up the pieces and begin to move forward. I continued in my own counseling, which I had actually begun ten years before and had discontinued. I don't think I was ready for all the pain I would have to feel. And, more importantly, I think on some level I realized that if I continued, it would jeopardize my marriage. My mother was an alcoholic, and my dad was incestuous. I had never dealt with any of that before.

A year before my husband left me, my brother went into therapy. Even though I still had blocked out what had happened to me, when my sister-in-law told me, I blurted out, "He was molested, wasn't he?" After that, I started crying a lot. I was tying into my brother's work. Prior to that time, I had shown very little emotion. In fact, in all the years I was married to my husband, I had never cried even once.

Well, therapy helped me work through all that stuff; all the memories started coming back, and I came to see why I had picked someone as emotionally isolated as my ex-husband. So not only did I have the grief of my divorce at that time, I also had all the childhood wounds and pain to deal with. It was really, really difficult. I did lots of crying, a buildup of thirty-seven years worth of crying. And the hard part was that I also had to keep an eye on the kids and get on with my life. At one point, I went to therapy twice a week to help me get through it all. I also attend Overcomers, a 12-step group at our church, which helped me, too.

In addition, I had a great network of girlfriends, and we'd get together and talk. One of them, who is also a neighbor, owns a restaurant with her husband, so she called me up every Saturday night and said, "You're coming with me." And we'd go out to dinner at their restaurant. I didn't want to go anywhere, but she kind of roped me into it. All my friends continued to include me in activities; they'd be sure to invite me to parties and things like that. My ex-husband is still angry that I kept my friends. He blames me for the divorce and thinks I should have lost my friends as a result. But I just tell him, "My friends have known me for a long time, some of them for almost twenty years, and they don't believe you when you say I'm such a bitch."

Actually, I think I'm a better friend now than I used to be. I was a real over-functioner before my divorce, so I had to put on this perfect image, perfect little house, perfect little kids. I put a lot of energy into making every-thing look really nice. Once I was divorced, I realized I couldn't pretend any-more; we are obviously not the perfect family, so in a way, it was a huge relief.

And my friendships didn't end, so obviously my friends weren't looking for me to be perfect. It became apparent that the message I had gotten from my parents—that I had better be perfect or else—was not true for everyone else. I noticed that my over-functioning was keeping people away. So after all the walls came down, I realized people were coming to me right and left.

One of my friends confided that she had been married before and that no one but her current husband knew. Another friend told me about an abortion she'd had. It occurred to me that all of these other people have problems and I certainly don't think any less of them, so they probably don't think less of me, either. It was this huge eye-opener.

In my family of origin, appearance was everything. At one point, when my older brother had tried to commit suicide, my parents kicked him out of the house. I decided that if I ever did anything wrong, I'd get kicked out too. So I became the "good girl," at least to them. Actually I was doing a lot of drugs at the time, though I never got caught doing that. As a result, I really split. I got straight A's in school, so they never suspected. It took me a long time to get back to putting the parts of me back together.

It's been more than three years since my divorce, and I have changed in so many ways since then. I am much more accepting of my flaws. Now there is not much I wouldn't tell somebody because I'm able to say, "I've made mistakes before, but I'll know better next time." So I'm more compassionate toward myself and others.

I don't think my ex-husband knows what to make of all this. I remember him coming over once, still in his blaming mode, saying, "You did this and you did that, and if your friends only knew."

"You can write all my sins on the garage door," I said, "because they already know." I could tell he was so mad.

Once I began to accept myself and quit trying to pretend as though I were perfect, I felt as though I lost all these chains. In fact, I had a dream about it one night—that I had all these chains on and they simply fell off. That's what a huge relief it was to me. When I was in therapy, I began writing a book, which has taken me two years to write, and it's not edited yet. But my attitude is: It'll get done when it's supposed to be done. And that's okay.

I'm less judgmental, too. Before, I wasn't able to look at my own feelings, so I know I wasn't able to look at others, especially my kids. In a way, I'm glad the divorce happened when my kids were so young. I know I parented them the way I had been raised—get good grades, be perfect. Now I'm more accepting of my children. I finally realized that I was really living under the law, and I continually felt God's judgment. I would carry it with me. So I really began to experience God's grace when I saw it enacted in my friends. That was a huge, huge thing because I had been really mad at God for the divorce. I felt like I had fulfilled my part of the law—I was a good wife, and a good mother, and a Christian—and God didn't keep His end of the deal. Now I'm more aware of God's grace; I'm able to live that out more in my life.

The hardest thing for me has been to learn how to set boundaries, and I'm still working on that. I'm more comfortable with it, but it's still not second nature. Before, when I'd set limits with my husband, he would just step over them and then I'd back away. It wasn't his fault because I could have set firmer limits; I just wasn't willing to face the confrontation. We were both very non-confrontational. In fact, when I was working on my master's degree, and I guess becoming more mature, I started to have an opinion about things, and he didn't like that. He used to say, "Guy, you argue a lot." But, no, I finally had an opinion.

Now I'm less willing to back down, or to take on responsibilities that aren't mine. Like last month, my ex-husband didn't take his weekend with the kids, and he said to me, "I didn't have a weekend [with the kids]."

"Did you ask for one?" I replied. "Did I say, 'No, you can't have one?'" I'm starting to realize that the more I set boundaries, the more comfortable I become. If I don't have the word "no" in my vocabulary, then my "yes" doesn't count. So I'm trying to balance not being selfish with meeting my own needs. Still, the hardest person to set limits with is my ex-husband. I end up feeling incredibly guilty. It's actually easier now with my parents than it is with him.

I also discovered that I could do a lot of things for myself that I didn't know I could. For instance, we always have a block party at Christmas, so I decided to still participate, but my ex-husband had always been the bartender, so I had to learn how to do the mixed drinks.

I'm glad we were able to stay in the house and that my ex-husband gave me custody of the kids. I don't think he wants the responsibility. He does see them four or five times a week. He'll take them to dinner, go to their soccer games, which is great, but that's the easy part of parenting. He also takes them one night a week, but my oldest daughter doesn't go very often, though my younger one does. I think that she has taken the divorce the hardest. She's the one most like her dad. He's very athletic, and so is she. One time, when one of her friend's dads moved away, she said, "I don't know what I'd do if my dad did that to me." I think she's afraid of losing her dad in that way.

So my divorce has really been a life-changing experience for me. I guess I've paid a price, in some ways, for all of this change because I view life less simplistically than I used to. I'm more willing to accept that there aren't always pat answers to everything. I find that kind of attitude sometimes sets me apart from some of the people at church, and it makes it hard for me to feel really connected at times. I remember when one of the ladies at a retreat found out about my divorce and she asked me if my husband and I had prayed together. I just couldn't believe her naïveté.

Looking back, I don't think we would have even known what to pray for! We were praying for help with finances and stuff, when the issues were so much deeper. I guess I'm less willing to put God in a box and pretend that I have Him all figured out. I'm more open to the possibility that I don't know everything and maybe things aren't always the way we think they are.

I'm still on this journey of discovery. I still go to therapy occasionally, though not as often as before. I'm working on my book, hoping to get it published. I'm open to marriage someday, and I'm in a relationship right now that I enjoy, but I'm not interested in getting married now. I want to be further along. I want to make sure I won't give away too much of myself like I did before.

REFLECTION

Karen's story shows how loss can be a catalyst for tremendous change. She describes how her "whole world had crashed" when her husband told her he wanted a divorce, and that is indeed what occurred. The carefully constructed old order of things must at times be demolished before something new can arise out of the ashes.

It is interesting to note that Karen had some awareness of what would be required of her when she decided not to continue in therapy ten years before her divorce. She was aware that to continue might cost her marriage and that was a price that she was not willing to pay. But events conspired against her, and when her marriage ended anyway, she was ready to once again take up the task that was calling her. That she chose to do so, knowing the depth of pain she would endure, is a testament to her courage.

Giving up the illusion of perfectionism, she learned that people love her for her humanity. She is free to be who she really is and can finally feel a measure of love and acceptance that she had denied herself. "You can write my sins on the garage door," she tells her ex-husband, "because they already know." She dreams of chains falling off her and feels the relief of being released from bondage.

Now Karen feels more connected to people, less judgmental and critical, more willing to allow for humanity and grace. Being more willing to accept that there are shades of gray means that she no longer feels the need to have all the answers, and to some degree this sets her apart from the women's Bible studies and prayer groups at her church. Patrick Henry, in his work, *The Ironic Christian's Companion,* notes that:

> To be both ironic and Christian is to know, with a knowing deeper than doctrine, the simple, unnerving truth that the visage of faith is not a happy face but the masks of comedy and tragedy, alternating, unpredictably, between laughter and tears, sometimes crying and laughing at the same time, or even, on occasion, crying because it's so funny and laughing because it hurts so much.[1]

This is the kind of faith Karen's journey has brought her to, one that includes a much larger vision of God, a more relational experience of the world, and at the same time a feeling of being apart from the group she once identified with. Her simple, childish faith has been tempered by pain, by loss, and by confronting the darkness. She has emerged into a new understanding of God that leaves room for mystery.

Faith is what underscores much of what has ultimately given meaning to the loss that each of the women in this book experienced. David Wolpe examines the role of faith in loss in his work, *Making Loss Matter.* "Why is this world built," he writes, "so that the seasons of life are shot through with autumn? There is no magic answer to loss. Nothing, not even time will make the pain completely disappear. But loss is transformative if met with faith."[2]

1. Karen's understanding of God changed as a result of her journey through grief in divorce. "I'm less willing to put God in a box," she says. In what ways have you seen your faith change as you move through your own divorce? When you compare your experience of God before your divorce and after, what is different? Write your answers in your journal.

2. Read Job 35:6–12. The Spiritual Formation Bible quotes St. Augustine as saying, "For the Omnipotent God, whom even the heathen acknowledge as the Supreme Power over all, would not allow any evil in his works, unless in his omnipotence, and goodness, as the Supreme Good, he is able to bring forth good out of evil."[3] Reflect on how good might come out of your experience of grief in divorce. What evidence do you have of this in your life or the lives of others? If you cannot yet see this possibility in your own life, pray for the wisdom to discern the beginnings of change when they do occur.

CHAPTER FIVE

One Divorce, Two Experiences

*It's not so long ago that my marriage cracked open on
a gray Christmas afternoon. That night, we raged at
each other like bruised animals, filled our glasses again,
and bellowed into the dawn, stripping away a past of
deception and pain.*

—ABIGAIL TRAFFORD

Crazy Time
*May it be said of us that we are Christians
who didn't always understand ourselves and
sometimes didn't even like ourselves,
but in our bones raged
the fire unquenchable that at last
consumed both our words and ourselves.*
—Calvin Miller
Into the Depths of God

In Chapter Three we explored the nature of grief as a phenomenon
that is common to all human experience. But, as anyone who has
gone through a divorce will tell you, grief in divorce is a unique and

79

complicated subcategory. To begin with, how and when you experience the grief of divorce depends on many factors but particularly on whether or not you were the initiator of your divorce. This is one of the reasons why divorce is so confusing. Just as there were two distinct experiences of the same marriage, there are two different experiences of the same divorce. Understanding these differences can help clear up some of confusion and also assist in navigating the grief process.

"I've been done with this marriage for a long time" — The process of grief for the initiator

It is often not clear who is the initiator of a divorce. Is it the person who files? The person who had the affair? The alcoholic who refuses to become sober? For our purposes we will say that the person who asks for the divorce is the initiator. The grief process for this individual is typically much longer than that of the non-initiator; and, as is the case with most types of grief, it can be better understood when divided into phases.

Phase One: Disillusionment

Though divorce is usually thought of as a singular event in time—once the divorce decree is signed by the judge—for the initiator it is a process that often begins in the earliest years of the marriage, usually with an experience of intense disillusionment with his or her spouse. This is not the normal disappointment that occurs when romantic idealization gives way to a more realistic perception, but it is rather more profound and deeply disturbing.

When this happens, the view of the spouse can shift dramatically. What once appeared to be a desirable trait is now seen as a problem. The husband, who at one time seemed easygoing, is now characterized as lazy or passive; the wife, who was seen as playful and fun-loving, is now viewed as careless and insensitive.

For a variety of reasons, disillusioned partners usually do not communicate their unhappiness directly. Instead, they will complain about something more mundane like the fact that their spouse watches too much television or doesn't spend enough time with the kids, when, in fact, the issues are actually much deeper. Sometimes this is due to a reluctance to hurt their spouse, or because the reasons for their unhappiness are vague and ill-defined. In addition, there is a prevailing cultural myth that the first year of marriage should be one long, happy honeymoon despite the fact that the vast majority of couples experience significant challenges during this time. This assumption, however, prevents people from seeking help during a time when it would be the most effective.

This was the case for Misty, who came to see me after years of trying everything she knew in order to make her marriage work. Even before her marriage, she had experienced serious doubts about marrying Steve, but she set these aside after an ardent courtship in which he worked hard to win her over. After they were married, though, he became more emotionally distant, working long hours to build a law practice and spending his weekends playing sports. When she would plead with him to spend more time with her, he would change his behavior for a few weeks but eventually drift back into his former pattern. During their first year of marriage, she seriously considered divorce, but her religious convictions, as well as the influence of her friends and family, overrode her concerns. Instead she went to physicians and therapists to treat the depression and anxiety that emerged.

Once their children came along, Misty was even more tenacious in her efforts to make their marriage work. At her urging, they participated in Marriage Encounter; they went to couples' therapy; they attended church together and went on couples' retreats. Nothing seemed to make a lasting change. Behind all her efforts, though, was Misty's essential belief that something must be wrong with her; if she were a better wife, lover, partner, then Steve would want to spend more time with her.

Phase Two: Despair and Discouragement

As Misty's story demonstrates, initially the disillusioned spouse feels tremendous optimism that eventually the partner will change and the marriage will get on the right track if they can only find the key. But when this doesn't happen, the disillusioned partner eventually gives up hope and instead tries to tolerate the marriage as it is. "Maybe I am asking too much of marriage" is a common thought during this time. Many of my clients come to see me at this stage; they arrive with just a glimmer of hope, but mostly despairing and discouraged. I hold the view that this emotional stalemate is an opportunity for personal and spiritual growth, a chance to change long-held assumptions and attitudes about relationships and to develop new, more effective responses.

Phase Three: Apathy and Indifference

For many people, however, the emotional distance continues to increase until the disillusioned spouse moves into the third phase of grief characterized by apathy and indifference toward their partner. Any sadness they might feel is for the loss of the hopes and dreams of what might have been, not for the loss of the partner or the marriage itself.

Sometimes the disillusioned partner will form some kind of transitional relationship, which can take the form of a new romance or simply a relationship with someone who has gone through a divorce themselves. Many individuals begin making specific plans for how they will live their lives once they leave. Others experience more ambivalence and vacillate between staying and leaving.

Phase Four: Decision to Divorce

Eventually the disillusioned spouse moves into the final phase and decides to initiate a divorce. This often is when the spouse realizes the seriousness of the situation and makes some attempt at changing. Sometimes they will make a frantic call to a therapist as a last-ditch effort to try to save the marriage. But in most cases this is generally viewed by the initiator, who by this time has little or no emotional investment left in the marriage, as "too little, too late."

Two sides to the equation

At this point you might be thinking that the non-initiator is to blame for the divorce. After all, if they had responded to the initiator's attempts to change, then things would have worked out. Or perhaps your sympathies lie with the non-initiator. If only the initiator had been clearer about their unhappiness early on, the non-initiator could have had a chance to save their marriage. As you can see, determining who is to blame for a divorce is not as simple as it appears and really not useful in any case.

The non-initiator often feels blindsided by the initiator's decision to divorce. Whereas the initiator has experienced unhappiness for years, the non-initiator can only see the clues of dissatisfaction in hindsight. This may be partly due to unclear communication with regard to the initiator's unhappiness in the marriage. Or it may have to do with the way this unhappiness was communicated.

In addition, initiators usually go through long periods of time when they are not overtly dissatisfied with their marriage. And even when they are unhappy they often try to ignore their dissatisfaction in hopes that it will simply go away. In these cases, the individual will distract themselves by becoming overly involved in work or child-rearing activities, thereby allowing the marriage to drift along

But it is not only the initiator's communication, or lack thereof, that contributes to the problem. It is also the non-initiator's inability to both notice and respond effectively to their partner's distress. These individuals tend to ignore or minimize difficulties, sometimes blaming their partner for "making a big deal out of nothing" or dismissing their problems as part of the normal experience of marriage. In many cases the non-disillusioned spouse responds by saying something like, "I'm happy in this marriage. Since you're not, there must be a problem with you."

In addition, once the disillusioned spouse enters the apathy stage and stops complaining, the non-initiator tends to interpret this as a good sign so that when the initiator finally says, "I'm through with this marriage. I want a divorce!" the non-initiator will exclaim, "But things were going so well!"

John and Maria came to me in this situation. John had recently moved out due to his long-standing unhappiness with the marriage, and Maria was completely blindsided by his decision. Though their marriage had frequently had its share of problems, Maria always thought they'd stay together. John, on the other hand, was emotionally burned out. He worked long hours in a successful business to provide well for his family and he was tired of coming home to a wife who nagged and complained. He was also concerned by what he saw as an increase in her outbursts of anger.

It turned out that Maria had also been unhappy for much of their marriage. She saw John as a workaholic who put work ahead of his family; she recalled many holidays where he'd show up to take pictures of the kids opening their gifts and then leave to take care of a client. "Though I worked hard to make our holidays special, we spent a lot of holidays without him," she recalled. Usually she tried to ignore her feelings of unhappiness and frustration, telling herself it didn't matter; but then, after months of stuffing down her feelings, she'd eventually blow up. For John, her anger seemed to come out of nowhere and was out of proportion to the situation. From Maria's point of view, it was the result of months of insensitivity on John's part.

Still, Maria had not seen John's moving out as a possibility and she was devastated. To make matters worse, it soon became apparent that John had started a relationship with another woman. As far as he was concerned, the marriage was over and he was moving on. Maria was now faced with the difficult task of grieving the end of a marriage that she still valued and treasured and the loss of a man whom she still loved.

"But I don't want a divorce!" — The grief process of the non-initiator

Maria's story highlights one of the most significant challenges of the divorce experience for the non-initiator. Lacking the time the initiator has had to let go of the marriage and create a new life, the non-initiator is left with processing tremendous feelings of grief, loss, and betrayal, while at the same time coping with the demands of separation and divorce. In this way, the non-initiator's process is more similar to that of a widow. But, unlike widows who have social support during their bereavement, non-initiators are usually left to handle their grief on their own.

One reason for this may be a societal assumption that the divorced person has failed at their marriage and thus does not have a legitimate reason to mourn. In addition, many people assume the marriage must have been so bad that the individual must be happy about the divorce. So even though the non-initiator will experience many of the feelings of loss and grief that those who are widowed experience, they will face the additional burden of processing feelings of shame and embarrassment as well as a lack of entitlement to feeling grief at all! Though the grief process of the non-initiator is different from that of the initiator, it too follows a predictable sequence of experiences.

Phase One: Shock and Disbelief

For most non-initiators, the news that their partner no longer wants to be married to them comes as a shock, accompanied by feelings of numbness, of unreality, of dissociation, as though one is watching a play. "This can't be happening to me," is the defining thought. This is particularly true if the breakup is experienced as sudden and coming out of the blue, but it is a common reaction even when there has been some kind of forewarning. Often, the non-initiator is able to discuss the impending separation with a great deal of rationalism, with the hopes that compliance might lead to reconciliation.

This was the case for Jennifer, who had been working with me for about a year in hopes of saving her marriage. Her husband, Ben, had come in for a couple of sessions but had lost most of his feelings of love and attraction for his wife and was unconvinced that these could be resurrected. Finally, one day Jennifer came in to tell me that Ben had moved out of the house and that they had worked out a visitation arrangement so he could still be involved with the kids. She was somewhat tearful but mostly appeared to be numb, as though the impact of his decision had not yet hit home.

Phase Two: Self-Blame and Hope for Reconciliation

After the reality sinks in, an intense feeling of grief emerges, and the mourning process begins in earnest, with all the concomitant symptoms associated with grief: appetite and sleep disruptions, impairment in thought processes, withdrawal from social contact, crying, and hovering by the phone in case their partner calls. Anger at the partner is typically unexpressed at this stage as the non-initiator attempts to preserve a positive image of their partners in case they return. Often this anger is turned inward as the non-initiator makes him or herself the scapegoat. Most non-initiators tend to focus on their own inadequacies and take the blame for the breakup. They spend hours reliving memories, sorting through events from the past that might help them make some sense of the present. Often, they are also receiving mixed signals from their soon-to-be ex-spouses, who, in a misguided effort to be kind, end up fueling the hope for reconciliation.

Jennifer went through this difficult phase soon after Ben moved out. He was not clear as to whether or not he wanted a divorce, stating that he just needed to be on his own for awhile. He would come by almost every day to pick up the kids and take them to school and often came over for dinner in the evening. Jennifer was unsure how to interpret these behaviors. One night they went out on a date and Jennifer felt very optimistic about their future reconciliation afterward. Later, though, she learned that his experience of their date was not the same as hers. He had felt awkward and ill at ease with her and saw this as further proof that their marriage should be dissolved.

Phase Three: Anger and Ambivalence

Eventually, though, rage does break through and hostile feelings will emerge. Now the non-initiator feels like a victim, and rage is directed at the initiator as the villain. The non-initiator becomes entangled in a web of feelings, vacillating between love, hate, and uncertainty.

In addition to anger and victimization, non-initiators often feel a great deal of fear, which can drive them to do anything they can think of to get their spouse to return to the marriage. They might become very accommodating and understanding, earnestly discussing issues, and they're often filled with erotic longing. Sometimes a sexual contact is initiated, but even if this is achieved, the results generally are not what the non-initiator had hoped for. Some non-initiators try dating others either in hopes that their partner might feel jealous and return, or, at the very least, to validate themselves as sexually desirable despite their partner's rejection. This courting phase generally ends when the non-initiators realize that no matter what they do, the separation will continue and it is futile to try to win their partner back.

Jennifer had been vacillating between hope and despair, rage and sadness, even before Ben moved out. After he left, and as more time elapsed, she became less angry but, conversely, all the more determined to keep the marriage together. She decided to let Ben make the first move with regard to initiating a divorce and, in the meantime, she would continue to live her life much as it had been before. While she longed for Ben to change his mind and return to the marriage, she was also aware that he had not been the husband she wanted him to be. Though she had been just as unhappy in the marriage as he was, she was not ready to pull the plug and file for divorce.

Phase Four: Distancing and Letting Go

In the next stage, the non-initiator begins distancing, as it becomes evident that continuing to hope for a relationship with their partner is futile. Now the non-initiator actively begins the work of letting go. Though feelings of caring for the partner still exist, the balance of power has shifted, and now the two are more evenly matched. Reconciliation is no longer taken for granted by either party; generally though, given the timing and behavior of the initiator, a resumption of the marriage still is possible.

Finally, if the initiator does nothing to encourage the non-initiator to resume hoping for reconciliation, the non-initiator will reach the last phase of the letting-go process and become indifferent. Letting go is now a relief and an emancipation. The former partner is now seen in a different light, someone who is alien, unknown, and no longer desirable. Often the non-initiator will wonder how he or she could have ever even wanted to stay in the union. The ex-partner is now, in the words of a song, "only someone that I used to love."

This was the case for Maureen, whose story you will read in the next chapter. As you read her story, notice the stages of grief that she experienced as she went through the process as a non-initiator.

1. In your journal, identify yourself as either the initiator or non-initiator. As you do so, be aware of the feelings that come up. Guilt? Shame? Anger? Despair? Write about your feelings and thoughts in a letter to God.

2. In his book, *Here and Now*, Henri Nouwen writes of the nature of God's love: "Maybe we still do not fully believe that God's Spirit is, indeed, the Spirit of love. Maybe we still distrust the Spirit, afraid to be led to places where our freedom is taken away. Maybe we still think of God's Spirit as an enemy who wants something of us that is not good for us. But God is love, only love, and God's Spirit is the Spirit of love longing to guide us to the place where the deepest desires of our heart can be fulfilled."[1] Where have you seen evidence of this in your life? Where do you see it now, even in the midst of your divorce? Perhaps it is in the friend who always has time to listen, or the concern of family members who offer to help. Take some time to contemplate this quote in a few minutes of quiet meditation.

CHAPTER SIX

New Beginning (Maureen's Story)

Goodbye to the Life I used to live—
And the World I used to know—
And kiss the Hills, for me, just once—
Then—I am ready to go.
—Emily Dickinson

I think I hooked up with my husband in a very naïve fashion. I had always believed that every problem could be solved, and I was a very hopeful person. I was completely unaware that some behavior patterns are very resistant to change. My husband came from a family that had a lot of emotional issues—extramarital affairs, a brother in rehab for a drug problem, a mother who acted out her pain on the kids. But I had no idea how this kind of upbringing would influence a person throughout his life.

I think I saw my husband's essential narcissism early on, but I thought that with maturity, he would change. I recall so clearly the words of a friend in college who said, "Maureen, he's got you on a pedestal and what's going to happen to you when you fall off?" And he really did idealize me to a large extent. The minute I walked into that science class, he told himself, *I'm going to marry that woman. Who is she?* And so he went after me with a very high level of intensity that at the time was very appealing.

I remember thinking, *This is somebody who is going to stick around. This is someone who is persistent, who is not intimidated by the fact that I'm a chemistry major.* So I looked at that behavior and overlooked the other issues, the lack of honesty, the immaturity that I really felt would change over time.

I had no way to know that being on a pedestal was such a burden, but I know that it's not what I wanted. I did not want to be worshiped. I did not want to be the most respected person he knew. I am a struggling human being, and I do the best I can. But I think his view of me was all a part of his desire for me to help him feel differently inside.

So in a large sense, both of us wanted the other to be different than we really were. He wanted me to somehow make him feel better about himself, to feel different inside than he did; I wanted him to be mature, able to put the needs of others, if not ahead, at least on a par with his own. Scott Peck talks about this, that after twenty years of marriage, you have a certain anger that this person is not who you wanted them to be and that you really have to work through that. And I think that was the case for both of us.

My husband was angry that I wasn't changing to meet what he wanted, that I wasn't making him feel the way he wanted to feel. I had gotten to the place where I had decided to live my own life and he could live his life too, but I really wanted to live it with him because I felt there were some things we could work on together. Even though my marriage was generally a lot of work, I think I would have stayed the distance if he had not decided to leave.

We essentially spent our twenties in school. He became a medical doctor, and I got my doctorate in biochemistry. During this time, we had three children and settled into our home. Because we had kids at such a young age, a lot of our time was spent being parents and a lot of our interactions involved parenting.

Our first big challenge occurred when I got a call from one of my husband's colleagues to tell me that he had confronted my husband about drug use. Apparently, he had been using for about six months. My husband told me that the drugs made him feel like all of his burdens and cares were releasing; he felt they made him calmer, though from my perspective, he'd just come home and fall asleep. I think he felt a certain level of social discomfort much of the time. In high school, he used alcohol and smoked cigarettes, so he had already experienced trying to use mood-altering substances.

Since I don't drink myself, I think he knew that I wouldn't be agreeable to his drinking at home, but his smoking continued behind my back, and periodically I'd find cigarettes in the car, which he would deny. Now I know these are signs of an addictive personality, but at the time, all I knew was that somehow I wasn't connecting with him.

As a result of his colleague's intervention, he voluntarily submitted himself to the medical board for a diversion program, which was good, and he went to counseling for about four years with a therapist whom we both respected. This counselor also helped us as a couple with issues that might come up with the kids, who were entering their teenage years. It was during this time that I learned about codependency.

In fact, that was the first time I had even heard the word. There was no doubt that caretaking was a part of my makeup, and that was what I knew to do. I was the oldest child in my family, which I think predisposed me to being responsible. My grandmother moved in with us, and, in the beginning, she was my caretaker. She made me breakfast in the morning and she was the person I came home to at night. But then she became very ill with cancer, and in some ways, the situation became reversed.

My parents were in their early thirties at the time, so they were relatively young, and I think they had difficulty coping with the situation. And while I in no way resented having her with us during that time, I do think that for a teenager, the emotional cost of caring for another person was awfully high. I was in high school, and my brother was a different personality who needed more attention than I did, so I think those factors fed into my being the overly responsible first child. I think I operated on an adult level too early on and that a lot of my caretaking tendencies stem from that experience. When I joined Al-Anon after my husband's addiction became apparent, I began to address my codependency.

In addition to counseling, my husband became involved in a 12-step program that he stuck with for at least seven or eight years. But then, he started backing off. He decided that he knew how he was feeling, and he told me that if he needed to go to a meeting he would go, but that he didn't feel he needed to go regularly anymore. Well, one thing I have learned about addiction is that it often switches from one thing to the next. In this case, he decided to go back to school for an MBA.

This was at the same time my daughter was starting high school, and I was opposed to his starting on a new degree. I just felt that it would be easier, especially since now we would have two kids in high school, if he would wait until they were out. But I didn't want to be the bad guy, so I left the decision up to him. I also let him know, however, that I wasn't going to be responsible for the consequences of his decision. His response was, "Well I'm always at the kids' athletic events, so what more can you ask?"

In retrospect, I realize that I felt really alone in my marriage. I had already spent my twenties living with him while he was being trained as a physician, and then he wanted to go into yet another program. It just seemed like too much. So we went to counseling for a few times around that issue, and the counselor said, "You know, it's okay to say, 'This will be the last degree.'" So I agreed to one more degree, because at the time it made sense, since he felt it would make him more employable. He started a program that would take four years to complete and then, after the third year, when our daughter went away to college, I discovered the affair.

In a sense, it was like another addiction for him. In fact, the way he talked about it was as though he were powerless over his behavior. He told me that she actively pursued him and when he didn't respond she started to verbalize her feelings and that's when he decided to respond. At that point, the level of addictive behavior in him was ten times worse than what I saw with the drugs. In his words, he was incapacitated, and I believe it because I saw it. In fact, my therapist just recently said to me, "Maureen, generally people who have gone through treatment for addiction end up leaving their marriage because they want to dissociate themselves from the experience." And I take that into account now when I tend to be overly hard on myself.

I found out about the affair through a bizarre set of circumstances. We had some difficulty with my daughter's email account not letting her know when she had a message, so, when I hadn't had a reply to one of my emails, I decided to check her account to make sure she had gotten it. I was checking my daughter's email and saw that there was a message on our computer that had not been sent and it was to an unknown address. So I opened it up, and it was just amazing for me to read.

Basically, I discovered that my husband was having an affair. At that point, he was on call at the hospital, so I called him up and said, "I found this email." We conversed off and on all night long; the next morning I called the therapist. I couldn't believe it. It was such an incredible betrayal.

In counseling, his focus was basically on how defective I was and all the reasons why he had the affair. "I've outgrown you." "You're controlling." "You love the kids more than you love me." "You've always wanted to change me; she accepts me the way I am."

My immediate response to the counselor was, "What do I need to do to change me? What do I need to do differently? How much validity is there in what he is saying? Am I controlling? Have I always wanted to change him? Have I not cherished him?"

After I waded through all that, I did admit to the things that I could have done differently. And I apologized for those things, and they are behaviors I don't want to repeat. I felt like that was a necessary thing to do on my part.

The counselor was really helpful to me during this time. I needed to be reminded of what was his responsibility and what was mine. I am not here to fill the holes in his life; I am not that powerful. In some ways, he found a woman who is really controlling. She is very aggressive. After he finally moved out, she stepped right in and made sure the papers were sent to the attorneys and to the forensic accountants.

Before that time, though, he spent about six weeks living in our house. I decided to allow him to be there as long as he needed to be; I wanted to be steadfast through the whole thing. But it got to the point where he was going out without me and not telling me where he was going, and I finally told him, "You know, you're right. You need to move out because this is just not healthy." I think that I allowed things to go as long as they did because I realized that separation usually leads to divorce. I felt that there was still some possibility for things to change while he was still at home. So I hung on to that as long as I could, but when he finally left, there was a certain relief.

When he left, he moved in with his girlfriend Rose right away. He moved out on Halloween, and by December, he called and said he didn't like living in limbo and that he had called a mediator. Before Christmas, I came home and found an envelope listing our belongings and estimating their value. It was obvious he and Rose had gone through the house and placed a dollar value on everything. It gave me such an unreal feeling. I mean, the violation of having another woman in my house evaluating my possessions was just an incredible affront!

He also began bringing Rose to church with him. The pastor asked me, "Maureen, is this true? I see your husband with this other woman that I assume is not his sister, and we're not going to have this."

So he told my husband, "You cannot show up at church with this other woman in front of your family, in front of your children. If you want to come by yourself that is fine."

To me it was such a clear example of how far above everything my husband and his girlfriend felt. It was like, "We're above it all. This is true love; we are invincible. We can do whatever we want to do."

In books like *Torn Asunder*, that's basically the attitude they describe. An affair creates an amazingly powerful connection—especially when you have a person with a tendency toward addiction, like my ex-husband. Once he left the marriage, he set everything in motion for a fairly rapid dissolution. In November of the following year, we hadn't even finished the legal aspect of our divorce when we had a bifurcation. That is where the marriage is dissolved, but the legal matters, such as division of property and custody matters, are still in limbo. Two weeks after the bifurcation, he got married.

That period of my life was incredibly difficult. Everything that was happening seemed so unreal. At the same time, a part of me was saying, "Okay, what do we need to do to fix this? What do we need to change? What do we need to solve?" I ultimately realized that the only thing I could work on was myself.

Dobson speaks of this tendency that when there is an affair, the one who is betrayed takes everything on. "I need to do this differently; I need to do that differently." And that is what I did. I really started looking at myself, probably in an overly critical way. I joined Overcomers at church, and because I had already been in Al-Anon, I was able to really build on that experience. In fact, I did a fourth step, in which you take a searching and fearless moral inventory. I spent about a year in Overcomers.

I also attended the divorce recovery workshop at our church, which was good because it provided material for how to get through a divorce. I also did my own personal therapy, which was especially helpful during the most painful months when I didn't know what my husband was going to do: Was he going to leave? Was he going to stay? My therapist really helped me with that, in a way that was specific to me and to what I wanted and needed. I went to my therapist at least once a week, sometimes twice if I needed to, so I could deal with all of the pain.

I also got a lot of support from both sides of my family, and that was really reassuring. I needed to talk to someone other than my therapist, so early on, I talked to my dad, and he talked to my mom. My dad helped me so much. He kind of gave his advice, which was helpful, because I was in such a state of confusion.

One thing my ex-husband's leaving did was stir up the pain of my other losses. So, for me, it came down to: "How much loss am I going to take?" Fortunately, I figured out what that was going to be, particularly with regard to my relationship with my ex-husband's family. I wrote them a letter and we had some conversations where I told them I wanted to retain my relationship with them in whatever form they'd like. They all came back and said, "We will keep our relationship with you," and that has eased the pain for me and the children. I'm sure it has probably made things more difficult for my ex-husband. While I am aware of that, at the same time I have decided that if I'm going to prioritize feelings here and whose feelings I am going to be concerned about, his are not going to be at the top of the list.

So initially, I really concentrated on myself and what it was that I wanted to do. But I was also aware of how this would affect my kids. For me, even though my marriage was a lot of work and ended the way it did, I wouldn't change it because I think I ended up with the best part of my ex-husband, our kids. That may be a kind of selfish way to look at it, but it's true. I have a wonderful part of him that I see in my kids, and so that part is really good.

For the most part, my ex-husband is not a big part of my life. I don't have to deal with him. My youngest son has been the most accepting and, because he spends most of his time with me, I think that has been helpful. He is now at the age where he is trying to sort out what kind of people his parents are. Sometimes he will parrot his dad's opinions, like when he mentioned that his dad had told him our marriage was over long before he divorced me and that his dad didn't start dating until after he moved out.

I don't say anything, and I find that he is able to consider other possibilities. I've requested that our youngest and his dad work out how much time they will spend together, which basically is a movie and lunch on two to three Sunday afternoons a month.

It's been harder on my two older children because they know they had been lied to. It was bad enough that he lied to me, but he lied to them, too. Both of them have confronted him, and then it got to the point where the response from him was one of anger—and they didn't want to communicate with him anymore. So they see him for dinner at Christmastime, and maybe for their birthdays. My daughter periodically decides to try and call him more regularly, and I think that's a good thing. The kids need to know who we are and not fantasize about either one of us.

I think the grief process didn't really begin for me until after the divorce was final. During the divorce, you're kind of forced into an adversarial role. So you spend a lot of time photocopying checks and financial records, and hoping your attorney can get you a fair settlement. You're being accused of things you can't believe you're being accused of. Things are being done that are dishonest. Papers are showing up that are falsified. So it's like one hurtful violation after another. But then, when you get through the divorce, you need to start to work on putting things back together, particularly yourself.

I think that not having any choice in whether or not I was divorced made it so much more difficult. It was really out of my control. And, in some ways, it seemed to come out of the blue. I have this letter from my ex-husband that I've kept that says he never wanted to be married to anyone else but me, and then three weeks later, he started his affair. That just reveals such a lack of honesty to me. And it helped contribute, I think, to the sense of unreality that I had initially.

But, in general, this whole experience has been a maturing process for me. I think that my addressing my codependency issues has been the area of greatest growth; I worked really hard on that in my therapy.

In the past, when there was somebody who did not like me, I would lose sleep at night. I moved from being unable to get to sleep to falling asleep but waking up in the night, to the point where I am today. Now I can say, "You know what? This person can be mad at me today, but tomorrow is another day." I can look at the situation and determine what the other person's part is and what part is mine. And if it's totally just their stuff, then I let them have their stuff! And I just go on. So it's much more a matter of getting rid of my feelings of inadequacy; now I tell myself, *This is who I am; there are areas I need to improve upon, but that doesn't mean I'm a bad person, or that I'm less than, because I'm not.*

So I'm much more accepting of myself, which makes me less judgmental of others. I've already broken through the perfection mold with my divorce. I don't run around trying to polish my image all the time. People are going to believe things about me that they want to believe, and though it's still pretty hurtful at times, I realize that, for the most part, it's out of my control.

At this point, I feel like I have choices and I'm not so weighed down, which I think was a result of my codependency. Now I'm very careful about what I'll take on and what I won't. I've found in my dating that most of the men still want a woman who is going to take care of them. And, in some ways, I think this view is supported by the church. (The belief that it's up to the woman to make the marriage work is so insidious.)

My relationship with God is more mature in many ways. At first, I was questioning. I'd say, "God, I prayed about this before I got married; where were You during that time?" But then I finally got to the point where I decided that God allows people to make their own choices, including the choice not to be what He wants them to be. And then, I wondered: *What's the point of praying?* Ironically, my kids have helped me in this area because they are so into discovering life and questioning the meaning of spirituality. My older son said to me, "Mom, I'm tired of these superficial prayers. It's like we're asking God to work harder!" So they push me, and I'm enjoying that part. I'm forced to think about these things, too.

My view of my ex-husband is that he is out there somewhere, but I do not seek him out. I stay out of his life, and I appreciate that he just stays out of mine. I have fantasies of meeting for coffee, but the person I want to have show up is not who he is! I'd like to get to the point where I feel about him as I would anyone else, but I haven't gotten there yet.

I wish I could get through an entire day without some conversation with him in my head, because I know I'm not in his head! So now, I just go ahead and do the mental exercises, *Okay, Maureen, this is something you want to communicate. How do we change that so it's something that you feel good about, that is working for you?* At some point, I do want another significant relationship, but it's not a priority; I want this old one to be finished first.

I have a lot to be grateful for, and I focus on that. It's helped me to learn to let go, and letting go of my ex-husband has helped me to start to let go of my kids in appropriate ways. And that's where I need to be. I'm entering into a new phase of my life because my youngest will be going off to college. So that will be another challenge for me. I'm sure that I'll be moving forward in one way or another in my personal and spiritual growth.

REFLECTION

Maureen's story reveals the way in which the naïveté of youth gives way to the wisdom of maturity. In youth, the ego reigns supreme. "I can do anything if I work hard enough at it" is the assertion of the young. The wise person knows that no outcome is guaranteed and that sometimes what we gain from an experience is not what we set out to achieve. All of Maureen's intelligence, competence, and diligence could not save her marriage. And this is the grief and betrayal of youth.

Ironically, betrayal is essential for consciousness and even redemption. From the first betrayal of infancy, when we discover that our mother is not really omniscient, we are propelled toward a greater awareness of ourselves. But in the seeds of betrayal, and all the pain contained therein, is the hope of redemption. Just as Christ's betrayal ultimately led to His resurrection, so, too, do we have the promise of a new life after a time of conscious suffering. This is the argument put forth by Jungian analyst Aldo Carotenuto in his book, *To Love to Betray*.[1] He maintains that the experience of betrayal is with us from the moment we are born; like the other elemental emotions of love, suffering, joy, and grief, it wounds even while it offers healing. Betrayal forces us to look at ourselves; it propels us into a reflection of our interior existence. Much like an encounter with death or suffering, betrayal offers us the opportunity to incorporate aspects of our psyche that we have disowned or cut off. Thus the movement toward individuation—toward wholeness as an authentic individual—is facilitated by betrayal.

All of the women interviewed for this book experienced this as they suffered the grief of divorce. Many, as did Maureen, recounted that they believed that they were less judgmental and perfectionistic. As a result, they felt more connected to other people, their children in particular. This is the outward manifestation of the internal shift. It is the reflection of the balance that has been brought to a previously one-sided experience of oneself.

Betrayal lies at the heart of divorce. It is the distinguishing emotion that separates the grief of divorce from other types of grief. For although it could be argued that the widow feels betrayed, on some level, by the death of her husband, in most instances, she is still comforted in the knowledge that he did not willingly choose to leave.

For the non-initiator of a divorce, grappling with the betrayal of the trust that is the fabric of a marriage, as well as the repudiation of vows that were meant to seal their relationship for a lifetime, is an arduous task. For many, the challenge is never really undertaken, usurped by the belief that a new relationship will suffice. For some, however, such as those who have shared their stories in these pages, the gauntlet is taken up and the challenge accepted.

For Maureen, the journey through grief came with its own unique and unexpected rewards. In this case, the loss of her marriage, and prior to that, facing the reality of her husband's addiction, served to redirect Maureen's focus away from an emphasis on the experience of others and onto an awareness of her own inner world.

The tendency to focus on the feelings and behaviors of others—to the detriment of one's self—is the core of what is meant by the term "codependency." The danger in doing so is that the person loses sight of who they are. Anne Wilson Schaef explains, "The lives of co-dependents are structured by the question, 'What will others think?'" She goes on to elaborate: "Their main goal in life is to try to figure out what others want and then deliver that to them, for co-dependents are people-pleasers. They have developed amazing abilities to learn about the likes and dislikes of other people, and they truly believe that if they can just become what others want, they will be safe and accepted."[2]

This is the essence of codependency: The feelings, wants, and desires of others take precedence over the individual's. It is a defense mechanism, a way to try to control the uncontrollable, to somehow guard against loss and emotional abandonment. But what Maureen discovered is that this behavior does not guarantee security or relational happiness; instead, it results in an alienation from oneself.

Now she is learning what it means to bring her true self into a relationship, whether it is with her children or her colleagues at work. She realizes that she cannot control what others choose to believe about her, however painful that may be, but she doesn't need to accept their assessment of her as the complete truth. "I can look at the situation and determine what is the other person's part, what is my part, and if it's totally their stuff, then I let them have their stuff!" she explains. "Now I tell myself, *This is who I am;*

there are areas that I need to improve upon, but that doesn't mean I'm a bad person or that I'm less than, because I'm not." She concludes that now she realizes she has choices and, as a consequence, is willing to live a more considered life with regard to how she spends her time and with whom she spends it.

Discovering one's authentic self is a by-product of a grief well-traversed. Each of the women presented in this work would attest that this is perhaps the greatest gift. Marilyn Jensen describes this assessment at the end of her account of her divorce:

> Nine years ago could I have known, I wonder, what lay in store for me when I had stood on this very spot and watched my old life leave? Probably not. Would I have chosen it? Probably not. Yet now I know that, however arduous, the destination was worth the trip. The lessons learned had strengthened me for the next leg of my journey, wherever it might lead.[3]

The use of the word "journey" as a metaphor for the grief experience—and indeed for life itself—implies a movement into unexplored territory. For some, this can be a terrifying notion, for the unknown can be treacherous. For others, though, this same idea conveys excitement and anticipation; for these people life is more than just a journey, it is an adventure.

O'Reilly, O'Reilly, and O'Reilly explain how external journeys often precipitate an inward shift in perspective. "Some journeys are destined to alter our lives irrevocably." And though they are speaking of physical journeys taken to other parts of the world, they are also aware that this same thing can be said of inward travels. "The ecology and topography of the inner journey is no less real than any other place we encounter 'out there' in the world-at-large."[4] Later, the authors quote Frederick Buechner, who describes this process:

> Whether we are rich or poor, male or female, our stories are all stories of searching. We search for a good self to be and for good

work to do. We search to become human in a world that tempts us always to be less than human or looks to us to be more. We search to love and be loved.[5]

This searching quality underlies the stories that are told in this book. For each woman, divorce was a catalyst toward exploration of their inner terrain.

1. The word "codependent" comes with a lot of emotional baggage, most of it negative. Generally it means we are anxiously focused on someone else in an attempt to keep ourselves safe. As a result, we end up losing ourselves in relationships. Review your own history of relationships. Is this an issue you have struggled with? If so, what might you do to try to change your responses?

2. Betrayal is an experience we all have at one time or another. Certainly this is an experience that is found in the Bible, particularly in Judas' betrayal of Jesus. Read Luke 22:47–60 three times. Read the words slowly and observe which phrase or word stands out for you. Ask God to reveal what He wants you to learn from this and then read the passage again. Observe anything that you may have missed the first time. Read the passage a third time and write down what you have learned about yourself.

CHAPTER SEVEN

Shame and Guilt

*When a marriage that is meaningful ends,
it is not like a lost tennis match or a business setback, it is more
like the death of someone once loved whom you have been a party
to doing in through betrayal, negligence, selfishness, stupidity or
whatever mode or modes of malfeasance and malpractice you committed your share of. What is needed is not to just do something
but to sit there with the guilt and the grief—to mourn and learn
and begin to atone.... Hence the need to experience fully the guilt
and the grief—the teaching feelings of a failed marriage.*

— TED SOLOTAROFF
"Getting the Point"
Men on Divorce

Guilt and grief are such painful emotions that it's hard to imagine that they can be teachers. But as Ted Solotaroff so wisely points out, if you are to wrest a blessing from the suffering that comes from the end of a marriage, you will need to "mourn and learn and begin to atone."[1]

This highlights the fact that guilt, and its kindred cousin, shame, are feelings that make the grief of divorce so different from other types of grief. Of all the aspects of grief that follow the breakup of a marriage, feelings of guilt and shame seem to be the most difficult to process for my clients, and they tend to re-emerge periodically long after the divorce is finalized. Thomas Jones, in *The Single Again Handbook*, poignantly describes his experience after his divorce: "Suddenly, I was feeling like a failure in almost every aspect of my life. I failed at marriage, and soon I began to feel like a failure as a father. Because I was in Christian ministry, I felt that I no longer had what it took to fulfill my calling from God. Therefore, I left the ministry and felt like a failure before God."[2]

Jones' experience is a common one for anyone struggling to come to terms with divorce, but perhaps all the more difficult for those whose religious tradition holds an intact marriage as the ideal. When Christians divorce, the normal experiences of guilt and shame are compounded by a nagging suspicion of spiritual and moral failure; not only have they let others down by their decision, they wonder if they have let God down, too. Christian writer Mary Lou Redding writes, "I had always tried as hard as I could to be a good Christian. I wanted more than anything to be a person whose life and beliefs match. . . . Admitting that I could not [make my marriage work] was admitting a personal failing as well as a spiritual one. . . . I had to admit that I could not control my life."[3]

So how can the failure of divorce—and most particularly, the guilt and shame that follow—be a teacher? In this chapter, we will explore the answers to this question and learn how wrestling with these emotions effectively can guide you to a deeper understanding of yourself.

Distinguishing between guilt and shame

Though closely related, guilt and shame are different in some significant ways. Guilt is usually the result of an act or behavior as in "I failed at marriage." Shame, on the other hand, has to do with value and worth as a human being: "I am a failure." Of the two, shame is arguably the most powerful emotion. This may be because shame is developed in the earliest phases of psychosocial development—between the ages of fifteen months and three years of age. During this time we learn to balance the need for autonomy with the need to remain connected with others. If we received loving and appropriate boundaries from caretakers, while at the same time being allowed to explore our world, we developed a firm sense of self.

This allows us to experience what some have called healthy shame, which develops when we were confronted with our all-too-real human limitations. This is an idea that John Bradshaw explores in his book, *Healing the Shame that Binds You.*[4] He argues that healthy shame can be the source of creativity and learning—and of spirituality.

In fact, without a sense of shame, we would be lacking in something that makes us fundamentally human. People who do not feel shame are called sociopaths. These are people who both repel and fascinate us, partly because they seem inhuman. We sense that something essential is lacking in a person who could torture and kill with impunity, feeling absolutely no empathy for the victim or remorse for their crimes. So it seems that shame, like so many of our primary emotions, is a double-edged sword. Without it we would not be human, even though there are times it can cause a great deal of unnecessary suffering.

As Ernest Kurtz points out in his book, *Shame & Guilt,* healthy shame is a consequence of our unrecognized perfectionism.[5] Sometimes it reveals itself in perfectionist assumptions: "I should never fail," or "I should never make a mistake." At other times, it shows up in the responsibility we feel for the problems of others, for the alcoholic brother who can't stay sober, for the adult child who can't seem to keep a job, for the mother with bipolar disorder who struggles with basic life tasks. It's as though somehow we have the power to make others happy, to get others to make good choices—as though we are God.

Thus healthy shame can help us to remember that we are not God. Ironically, this can be a challenge for Christians who may have slipped into an unconscious assumption that if they live a good life, they will avoid pain and suffering. This is a denial of the truth that we do not control the outcomes of our lives. As the Bible reminds us, "The rain falls on the just and the unjust."

An example of this can be seen in Karen's story as she recalled her response to her husband's decision to file for divorce: "I had been really mad at God for the divorce. I felt like I had fulfilled my part of the law—I was a good wife, and a good mother, and a Christian—and God didn't keep His end of the deal."

And Karen is not alone in her assumptions. We are all a razor's edge away from paganism, in which the gods are expiated by our own endeavors. It feels so much more comfortable to think that we have the power to control the uncontrollable by maintaining a bargain with God. It is so difficult to live with the mystery of a God whose ways are higher than our ways—the suffering God who died on the cross, the God who is revealed in the poor, despised, and marginalized.

This is what a divorcing Christian can learn from confronting the shame of divorce: The realization that God's grace is greater than our behavior, our decisions, our mistakes, our transgressions, and that Jesus willingly assumed the limitations of human nature and urged others to do so as well. His Sermon on the Mount centers on the idea of learning to accept what is and let go of what cannot be controlled. "Let today's own troubles be sufficient for the day," He exhorted.

Like shame, guilt also has its healthy and toxic variations. Healthy guilt lets us know that we have transgressed our own value system—we have violated our moral boundaries. Guilt is the guiding emotion in determining our moral and ethical standards. Just what those standards should be has been a matter of speculation throughout human history.

In our modern era, Lawrence Kohlberg spent many years studying how human beings develop a sense of morality. Out of this research, he created a scale of moral development that has at the highest level the ability to act out of internal values. A person at this level holds others in regard, is capable of empathy, and is committed to justice for all.

Similarly, James Fowler has studied faith development in which he describes the final stage as characterized by universal compassion and concern. It is striking to me how these characteristics are so clearly evident in the life of Jesus whose final act of compassion resulted in the sacrifice of His own life. It could be said, then, that guilt is part of the process of spiritual formation whose end result is that an individual no longer is motivated by guilt but by compassion.

On the other hand, guilt can become toxic when it is diffuse and pervasive; a person with this type of guilt usually feels guilty much of the time and cannot identify the reason. The key distinction between these two types of guilt is that healthy guilt can be atoned for—you can do something to make things right; whereas, toxic guilt is never-ending and there is nothing you can do to right the balance because the guilt is not about a particular act or behavior. Much like a smoke detector that goes off every time you light a match, this kind of guilt ceases to be of use to the individual as a moral indicator. This is what is called neurotic guilt.

Individuals who struggle with neurotic guilt often find it very difficult to accept feedback from others—they tend to be overly touchy and defensive. This is because they are already so hard on themselves that hearing criticism from others is too much to bear. This defensiveness, in turn, makes it difficult for them to hear someone else's pain and frustration. So, rather than being useful in maintaining good relationships, toxic guilt actually contributes to tearing them apart.

Processing feelings of guilt and shame

In the not-so-distant past, individuals had recourse to rituals like the rite of confession in the Roman Catholic Church where they could confess their transgressions to another person, one who carried religious authority. They could also perform some kind of act to atone for their transgression. Though those of the Catholic faith still have access to this rite—now called the rite of reconciliation—it has become less commonly utilized. For those outside the Catholic faith, little is available to formally confess and atone. The closest to this ritual is found in the twelve steps of AA in which individuals make a "searching, moral inventory," "humbly ask God to remove [their] defects," and "[make] amends whenever possible" to those who have been harmed by their actions.[6]

Psychotherapy is another means by which individuals can learn to release themselves from the grip of neurotic guilt while at the same time respond appropriately to the feelings of healthy guilt. In the place of a formal, overarching religious belief system, psychotherapy is often the only

way in which individuals can learn to confront themselves and to distin-
guish between true guilt and neurotic guilt.

Shame and guilt are such primary human emotions that they can be
seen in one of the first stories in the Bible as Adam and Eve are tested by the
serpent and yield to the temptation to transgress God's command. Immediately after tasting the forbidden fruit, both Adam and Eve realize they are
naked and cover themselves. This is the picture of shame: We seek to hide
our true selves from others. But in this case, the shame is the result of an
actual transgression and is thus interwoven with guilt.

And in typical human fashion, as soon as their sin is found out, the
blaming begins. "The woman you gave me," "the serpent"—basically, "Don't
blame me!" How difficult it is to own up to our transgressions and how easy
it is to point the finger at someone else.

But without a sense of shame, there is no boundary to our tendency to
seek to be like God. Without a sense of guilt, there can be no repentance,
no turning away from behavior that is harmful to self and others, and no
movement toward inner growth and development. So in this vein, shame
and guilt can be valuable emotions, necessary if we are to stay in right connection with ourselves, others, and with God.

Learning from feelings of shame and guilt in divorce

Knowing that, then, how do you make use of the shame and guilt you
might feel in the aftermath of a divorce? The answer to this is just as complex as the emotions themselves. I recommend that you start by noticing
when you are experiencing either of these feelings and then jotting down
the thoughts you are having at that moment. You can do this either by
keeping a pad of paper handy and writing down the thoughts as the feelings arise, or by setting aside some time to contemplate your divorce. For
instance, you might think, *I should have tried harder in my marriage* or *I feel
embarrassed about telling my friends at church that I'm getting a divorce* or *my
kids are going to be scarred for life!*

Sometimes it helps to visualize a scene. For instance, you might think about telling the members of your women's Bible study that you're getting a divorce and notice that you feel mortified as you imagine their reactions. Ask yourself, *What am I telling myself?* It could be something like, *They'll think I'm a failure,* or *they'll want me to leave the group,* or *I can't face them!* Do the same for other situations you may have to face: telling your parents and siblings, telling your children, writing "separated" or "divorced" on an application form.

You'll want to keep track of your thoughts and feelings for about week in order to get a clear picture of the typical situations and thoughts that bring about feelings of shame and/or guilt. If this sounds distasteful, keep in mind that you're already having these thoughts and feelings; you are just not keeping track of them. In so doing, you'll be moving toward consciousness of your own experience, which in turn will assist you in learning what you need to learn.

Once you complete your list, see if you can identify which feelings are shame-based and which arise out of guilt. Shame-based feelings generally will bring about questions about your own worth; embarrassment is an indication of shame. Guilty feelings will be more closely tied to behaviors; the impulse often follows to try to make up for something you've done, to make amends.

Next, take two pieces of paper. Label one "Shame" and the other "Guilt." Then draw a line down the middle of each. On the left side of each paper, write down the thoughts you have identified. Once you have done this, try to come up with a response that is more factual. If you can, find a Bible verse to support this truth.

Put yourself in the mind-set of a loving, nurturing parent. Perhaps you can imagine you're talking to your child who has just told you they are getting a divorce. If your son or daughter added, "I'm such a failure; God can never forgive me," you wouldn't say, "You're right!"

More than likely, assuming you are a kind and loving parent, you would say, "You may be feeling bad right now, but God's love is unconditional. In fact, He wants you to stay closer to Him now than ever before. Yes, your marriage did not work out, but you're taking the time to learn from this." Continue to do this for each thought you have listed on the page.

Now, review your list and see if there are any actions or behaviors that you can make amends for. For instance, let's say you feel guilty for yelling at your ex-spouse in front of the kids. Take some time to prayerfully consider how you can respond to this in a way that would bring healing to all concerned. Perhaps a letter of apology might say something like: "Dear John (or Susie), I know this divorce has been difficult for all of us. I want to ask your forgiveness for the times I lost control and yelled at you. My intention is to move forward and parent our children together as positively as possible."

My prediction is that this would be one of the most difficult things you have ever done, and more than likely you will want to put that aside as a terrible recommendation. "You don't know my ex-husband or ex-wife! They'll just take advantage of me or they'll just throw it back at me next time."

This is where you will need prayerful consideration. If God calls you to do this as an act of Christian love—for yourself and your ex-spouse—He will give you the strength to write it. If you do so, remember that this is something you are doing for yourself in order to learn, grow, and be healed from the wounds of divorce. It is for your own spiritual formation. Thus you will want to keep your eyes on God and focus on your own self—not on the reaction of your spouse.

Mary Lou Redding speaks of this as she worked through the aftermath of her divorce: "Forgiveness is the only way to deal with hurts and get free of them. It sounds simple to do, but forgiving is often a long and wrenching process. It is a process rather than an event or an act. Even deciding that we ought to forgive can take time. Who wants to forgive someone who has inflicted hurt on them year after year? We may feel that it's not fair to absolve others. But if we merely exile them as David did Absalom, if we only put them out of our mind and do not face the issues between us and them, we remain tied to them emotionally."[7]

In making amends for those behaviors and actions that have been hurtful to others—or that were not in keeping with our values for ourselves—we are opening ourselves up to healing and blessing. It is similar to the Navajo tradition of balancing out the community by making up for deeds done against one of its members with a counterbalancing act. Ms. Redding describes a conversation a friend started after the divorce:

"There's always sin in divorce."

"What do you mean?"

"I mean that we are sinful people, and because we are, we end up getting divorced. We disobey God by doing things we know we should not. That is sin."[8]

This takes us to our next step, based on the 12-step model of a "searching and fearless moral inventory," which itself is derived from spiritual principles. In order to learn what you can from the experience of divorce, it is necessary to learn about your contribution to your divorce. This does not mean that you take full responsibility or blame for the divorce—even if you were the person who initiated it; it means that you examine the patterns of your behavior in your marriage to see what you can glean in terms of self-understanding and insight.

In Ms. Redding's case, she heeded her friend's suggestion and decided to examine the ways in which she had missed the mark—to use another term for "sin,"—during her marriage. She identified several, including arrogance for not being willing to take some premarital assessments their counselor had recommended, as well as disobedience and cowardice for not listening to her own grave doubts in the weeks before her wedding. "My pride kept me from hearing what God kept saying," she reveals.[9] This was indeed a fearless and searching inventory, and she responds to each either with a prayer for forgiveness or, if applicable, a letter of apology and request for forgiveness from someone else.

You may want to create a prayer that you can use during this exercise in which you ask God to grant you courage to face your shortcomings, the grace to receive His forgiveness and the wisdom to know how to respond to this knowledge. Keep in mind that this is meant to release you from the burden of shame and guilt, to "mourn and learn and begin to atone."

Once you have done this, remember that Jesus died for your sins and paid the price for your transgressions. To hold onto them after you have atoned and asked for forgiveness will cheapen the value of His tremendous sacrifice. Our next story reveals how healing forgiveness was for Joan and the long and arduous journey she took to get there.

1. Take some time to do one or two of the listed exercises. You may want to start with the first and work through each one in order. Write about your experiences with these exercises in your journal.

2. The feelings of shame and humiliation are often linked together, but unlike shame, humiliation can have spiritual implications. Humility connotes having one's feet on the ground, of being clear on one's assessment of oneself. To be humble in the true sense of the word means that you accept yourself as you are, without comparison to someone else. In your journal, write a description of yourself without judgment, using the lens of God's love and grace. If you have a hard time with this, think of how you might write about one of your own children or someone else whom you love. See yourself through that perspective.

CHAPTER EIGHT

Letting Go (Joan's Story)

To live in this world
you must be able to do
three things:
to love what is mortal;
to hold it
against your bones knowing
your own life depends upon it;
and when the time comes to let it go
let it go.
—Mary Oliver
New and Selected Poems

I think that for many years, I lacked the courage to stand firm on my beliefs; as a result, I compromised myself too easily. I believe that my longing for acceptance and love was so strong that I allowed myself to be manipulated by others, particularly those that I cared for. The biggest example of that was when we were planning our wedding and my fiancé, now my former husband, said that he didn't believe in God and that he strongly objected to having God mentioned in the ceremony. Well, I had become a Christian in high school and this was something that was really important to me. But I said, "Okay, if he has such a strong opinion about it, I won't provoke him," when in fact, my heart was aching.

I had already learned by then that to express my opinion would mean a heated battle, so I decided to choose the path of least resistance, and devalued myself in the process. Now I look back and realize that I didn't believe in myself as being worthy and deserving of respect. Also, I was too afraid that if I really looked at our relationship and stood firm in my beliefs, we would break up. And that was terrifying to me. There were a lot of red flags about our relationship that I didn't pay attention to when we were dating: his angry outbursts, his disrespect toward me. I turned a blind eye because it would have been too scary to me to end the relationship.

After we got married, we both wanted to pursue additional schooling and then build our careers. Our plans did not include the possibility of having children. Again, I remember thinking that someday I'd like to have a family, all the while knowing that this was far from my husband's mind. Whenever I would bring up the subject, my husband would say, "I'm not sure I ever want to have children." And because I was afraid of recognizing the truth of what he was saying, I'd put my decision on the back burner and not continue the discussion.

Within a year, we decided to move from the East Coast to California so we could spend time pursuing our hobbies. This moved us far away from both our families and all of my friends. I didn't have a job for quite some time, and shortly after starting his new job, my husband became unhappy and complained constantly.

In many ways, I think that was the point when we started to separate. He became irritable, judgmental and quick-tempered. As I discovered the excitement and fulfillment of a new job, I began to spend long hours at work. The only thing that brought us together was working on our house on the weekends. That was our common interest. But that was also really stressful.

We had difficulty making decisions together. My husband insisted on doing everything himself, but was often too tired to work on the weekends. As a result, it ended up dragging on for a really long time. I remember that my kitchen had a dirt floor for two years! After a while, our jobs became an escape from responsibilities at home and a relief from each other.

We started looking to other people rather than each other for friendship. My husband had only two close male friends, but he did develop these very, very close relationships with a couple of female coworkers. They weren't sexual, but I think they drew some of the emotional energy out of our relationship. I developed a few close friendships with other women through work, but over the years they changed jobs or moved. That's when I really started to see that my husband wasn't there for me.

I don't think I ever felt completely comfortable around my husband. I realize now that throughout much of our marriage, I was living in fear of his anger. He was very volatile, and I was very good at placating. I don't remember a lot of fighting, but for the most part we were living as housemates. We were connecting less and less—including sexually, especially after I mentioned my strong desire to have a child. A year later, I did get pregnant. He has since said that he did that to pacify me, not out of any desire to connect with me.

Even so, things seemed to change for the better around that time. About a year before the birth of my son, I began to reconnect with my spiritual life and I started attending a Friday morning Bible study before work. My life began to change.

I found a church that I began to attend, and my husband began to talk about starting his own business. We had always shared the desire to be self-employed. I felt so excited about this change in direction, although I did sense that my husband was disturbed by my renewed faith.

We bought a plumbing-related business and it quickly grew. I remember thinking, *I've got it all now.* My husband and I seemed to connect a little bit closer; we had this baby boy, and even though we didn't get to spend a lot of time with him during the week, we had the weekends together and I thought things were improving. We were feeling some stress because the business required a lot of our time and energy, plus we now had an infant.

Nevertheless, at that point, I was hopeful. I started discussing the idea of having a second child. So we talked about it, and I thought we were in agreement on it, and I became pregnant. But in counseling, I later learned that he felt really hurt and angry about my becoming pregnant and he told me I had tricked him.

Toward the end of my pregnancy, we attended a convention that in many ways was the last shining moment of my marriage. But even then, I remember a bit of a foreshadow of what was to come. During a workshop on exercise, my husband boasted about how healthy he was and how together he was, and I remember thinking, *That's not true. What he is saying is not true.*

It was shortly after we came home that he became extremely ill. He went out on a job that was two and one-half to three hours from our house and came home with a cut on his finger, which quickly became seriously infected. Then other unusual symptoms, like lower back pain, appeared. He ended up being hospitalized. From the beginning, the doctors were puzzled and some thought it was a psychological reaction due to the pressure of his work and the additional responsibility of a second child. Eventually the doctors decided it was transverse mellitus which is a wastebasket term for a viral infection located in his spine.

However, after five MRIs, the diagnosis was still unclear. He became semi-paralyzed, and though he could walk, his mobility was restricted, and at times, was painful. I was about nine months pregnant at this time and sick with a bad cough when I went in to see my doctor for a checkup. To my surprise, my water broke after a hard cough and my doctor sent me to the hospital. *Great timing!* I thought. *My husband is in the hospital; I'm sick. I have a toddler at home, and we have a business to run.* I drove myself to the hospital and walked into my husband's room. "Guess what. We're having a baby today," I announced. They wheeled me into the delivery room and I had the baby. We never, never pulled ourselves back together from that point on.

Things got worse. Though my husband's health improved considerably, he had a relapse after three weeks. He was put on a large dose of steroids to be administered at home. The side effects from the drugs were horrible. My husband became paranoid, had severe mood swings and extremely angry outbursts, though he was able to function fairly well in our business with the help of his brother.

And here I was with a newborn and a toddler, and, except for his brother, with very little outside help. I was in pure survival mode. I knew that we had a lot of problems, but I couldn't even begin to address them at that time. My husband's behavior became so extremely unpredictable and abusive that I moved back East for two and one-half months. We spoke every day, but our communication was strained. I found out later that he was having an emotional affair with a customer.

Eventually, we went to see a psychologist about our marital problems, and my husband went to her a couple of times on his own. The second time we went to see her together, she said she wanted to see me alone. She asked me if I knew that he wanted a divorce. This was a complete surprise to me, though I found out later that everyone in my neighborhood knew he wanted a divorce. Apparently, the emotional affair had become more than a friendship. She was going through a divorce, and I think she really fed into whatever anger he had.

Anyway, everything began to unravel. Here I was, trying to be a mom to my two very young children, handling the responsibilities of a house and home and unemployed, and now I was going to face life completely on my own.

But the wonderful thing about this is that it put me on the floor, just crying out to God. And I had to do it; I had to go through losing my husband and my dreams in order to bring me to the place I am now. At that point, I had two purposes in living: one was to train my two children to know the Lord Jesus Christ, and the second was to get myself emotionally healthy enough so that my children wouldn't need to repeat the same relational pattern that I had followed.

I started attending a Christian 12-step program called Overcomers during that time that was really instrumental in helping me to work on my stuff. I started asking God, "Who do You want me to become?" rather than focusing on what this other person wanted me to be.

In the past, because I didn't believe I was worthy and deserving of respect for just being me, I would kind of mold myself to the other person. My inherent desire is to be a people-pleaser and to want everybody to like me, so my focus was always on the other person. When I found myself alone, I began to ask myself questions like, *Why did I find myself with such a person?* or *Why am I making these choices in my life?*—that type of thing.

I also learned how to express my feelings. Before, when somebody asked me, "Well, how do you feel about that?" I didn't have any words to tell them. I had denied my feelings for such a long time that I couldn't put words to my feelings; I just knew that I didn't feel good. But now I have so many more words available. During this time, I also went into individual counseling, which helped me find some of the answers to my questions.

I think the fact that I had two children motivated me to work faster and harder on healing and becoming healthier. I strongly desired to give them a different kind of heritage than I had. In some ways, we were on this journey together. I searched high and low for a poster that says, "How are you feeling today?" that has pictures of faces to go with feeling words. Now I have it on my bathroom wall so my children and I can refer to it when we need to.

It's been a difficult thing to learn to express myself in that way, and to feel safe doing so. But I'm learning—and my children are learning—to put the face to the emotions. I remember when I was going to court one time and a friend who went with me for support pointed out that even when I was upset with my lawyer, I had a smile on my face. She said, "Your words expressed your anger, but you had a smile on your face." I realized then that I needed to learn that feelings of anger are okay at times; my body language and words needed to match.

In addition to Overcomers and counseling, I attended a divorce recovery workshop, which was really useful in helping me sort things out. I started out as a participant and then volunteered as a leader. I grew a lot and I began to share with others what I had learned. I was on a real journey of discovery and growth, so I didn't stop reaching out to people. I talked to people. I surrounded myself with people—single, single parents, elderly, and children—and I found it very healing and helpful to be vulnerable and to express my emotions: anger, disappointment, relief, sadness, guilt, loneliness, anxiety, and shame.

My children had some counseling, too, which was really helpful. In particular, my son was really feeling pulled because my ex-husband's and my lifestyles are so different. He got a wonderful word picture from his counselor that helped him to identify an emotion he was obviously experiencing. She said something like, "What you are experiencing is like being in a car crash."

That taught him to be more in touch with his feelings and to say, "I don't like it" by saying to me or to his dad, "This feels like a car crash to me." His dad and I were also instructed and counseled individually by our son's counselor, which was extremely beneficial. At this time, my husband was still refusing to be anywhere near me, but at least we had a shared interest in our children.

I think that as a result of this divorce experience, my children are so much more knowledgeable than I was at their ages. I know they know what suffering is, and my hope is that they will be very compassionate people as a result. They know the dark side and they know the light, and they know they have a choice between the two. I'm much more accepting of my children, too. I have a quote on my refrigerator door that says, "It doesn't matter." Over and over again, when I'd have little patience, I'd refer to that quote and could let go. This quote helps me keep my perspective and choose what is truly important to respond to. Together, we are in a process of learning and growing, which I expect will last a lifetime.

I continue to try and look at life through their eyes because I didn't grow up with divorced parents. Also, in many ways, I've learned to detach from them, too, in a healthy way. At first, it was so hard for me when they would go to their dad's for a weekend. But now, even though it's still hard to kiss them good-bye for two days—and some Fridays are harder than others—I'm grateful for the time alone. I've learned to do a lot of self-talk, acknowledging my feelings and expressing them to safe friends in my life and then letting them go.

I still go through the exercise in my mind of imagining a large sack lying in a house, filling it full of all my negative emotions, placing it on a conveyor belt, and sending it away. If the sack returns, I immediately put it back on the belt! I began to cherish those weekends. It's a wonderful break for me and gives me the opportunity to take care of myself and do activities that I might not have done otherwise.

Even though I've experienced many, many changes in the aftermath of my divorce, I truly feel that my biggest breakthrough came when I was able to love and forgive my former husband. For most of my married life (13 years) and even after my divorce, I wore a breastplate and he carried a sword. His severe anger and spirit of revenge forced me into court for six years, mostly over child custody issues as they related to finances. He dragged me into court over the most petty issues, and my attorney became frustrated and ineffective against his outbursts in court.

I found it difficult to find a lawyer I could trust to end the battles. It was hell: the psychological evaluations I had to go through, the depositions. Once, when he was acting as his own attorney, he was the one who took the deposition from me, which should never have happened.

And, of course, the kids were drawn into it. He'd try to get back at me through them. When it was his weekend, I'd set up a time to call our children, but when I'd call, he wouldn't answer the phone. Weekends weren't as tough as when they'd stay with him for a week or so. Over and over again, I had to learn to deal with severe heartache and sometimes I would crumple into a heap with many tears. My husband's anger manifested itself in very hurtful ways.

Then something happened inside me and I realized that I needed to pick up my sword—God's Word—and live it. To me this meant that I needed to choose to love my former husband more than I had ever loved him. Not with the kind of love one has for their husband, but with agape love—the kind Joseph had for his brothers even after they left him to die. One spring I spent six weeks calling my ex-husband every couple of days, asking him to consider getting together to talk about his plans with the children for the summer. It wasn't easy because so often he was verbally abusive. Only through relying on God's strength could I persevere.

Finally, after six weeks, he agreed to talk on the phone. I prayed and trusted in God's guidance. He was faithful, and our conversation went well. I decided to put on the full armor of God and trust that God will take care of my children in whatever situation they are in. Now, whenever we talk, I rehearse the following thoughts: I am a child of God (I have value); everything is negotiable; and the phrases, "let me get back to you," "that's interesting," and "this is what I believe." When I remind myself of those things, it's like I am arming myself in a positive way to stand my ground without being disrespectful to him or to myself.

I can still feel and still have emotions; I still have the painful memories, like when my husband was moving out and my little son asked, "Daddy, don't you like me anymore?" I still cry when I remember that. But I can love my ex-husband now, not as a husband, but as a fellow human being. That doesn't mean I necessarily like him, or approve of his lifestyle, but that I no longer need to respond to him defensively. I have learned to empower myself and my fear of how he may behave is gone.

It took me about seven years to get to this place. I remember in the divorce recovery workshop that one of the speakers said that on average, it takes about half as long as you were married to go through the healing, and that's what it's been for me. Now it's no longer about the other guy, my ex-husband, or anyone else for that matter; it's about me: What are my values and principles, and how do I want to react?

Ironically, dating after my divorce also helped me grow as a person. When I first started dating, after all the work I had done on my own growth, I thought that the next relationship would be different from any of my past ones.

But then I got into a relationship that lasted about two years; it was back down the same road again—different guy, same characteristics. However, this time I recognized the red flag, the red flag that showed he was not interested in changing or looking at his anger. He would say, "Jesus loves me just the way I am" without adding the second part: "but He's not going to let me stay that way." Instead, he'd say, "You're going to have to love me just the way I am, even though I scream and yell at you."

But this time I said "No." And I ended the relationship. Going back through this a second time and having to break it off was hard because I had really let my heart go, but the experience made me see that I have more to learn. Then, when I date again, I'll see those red flags right away. I just know when I meet the right man, I am not going to have to work so hard; I'm not going to settle for less than I deserve. I'll be able to bring all of who I am into the relationship. I'll have so much more energy for the rest of my life. And that is worth waiting for. It's something that I am looking for, but not in desperate need of. "Let go and let God" is really what it is all about for me.

Now I am working in a career that I know I wouldn't have had I not gone through the divorce. I am truly following my passion, and God is opening up doors for me I never would have dreamed of. I'm learning that you don't stop growing; you don't stop therapy—either through an accountability group, Bible study, or even a 12-step program. I never want to stop growing and learning. My heart's desire is to be more like Jesus. I don't have that longing to be loved and accepted by everyone. I am determined to live my life standing firm in knowing that Jesus loves me. That, for me, is the greatest gift of all.

REFLECTION

Joan began her adult life fearful of the cost of authenticity. She relates that her longing for acceptance and love was so strong that she allowed herself to be manipulated by others. In the face of loss of love, she chose to remain silent and betray herself in the long run. The phrase "courage of one's convictions" underscores the threat of loss that standing up for one's beliefs entails. Just as Karen had been reluctant to pursue therapy for fear of losing her marriage, Joan was afraid that informing her fiancé of the importance of her Christian faith might end their relationship.

But, as both women learned, they were simply postponing the inevitable. The psyche abhors inauthenticity; the truth about oneself is bound to come out, whether through conscious choice or unconscious behavior. When Joan reconnected with her spiritual life, she was called to begin a descent into a time of great pain and loss of the very relationship she had sought to hold onto.

Finally, she came to the end of herself. "But the wonderful thing about this is that it put me on the floor," she relates, "just crying out to God. And I had to do it; I had to go through losing my husband and my dreams in order to bring me to the place I am now." This story of death to self in order to find life is one that is echoed in the story of Joseph to which Joan alludes in her portrait. That story is the one most frequently referred to by the women in this study. Joseph's loss—of his family, his position, his way of life—feels kindred to the loss these women experienced in their divorces. Likewise, his time spent enslaved, followed by long years in prison, echoes the period of grief, the dark time, that followed. For many of these women, Joseph's willingness to forgive his brothers for the betrayal was also significant. "You intended to harm me, but God intended it for good to accomplish what is now being done," explained Joseph in Genesis 50:20. His experience had deepened and prepared him for the task that he would later take up as second in command to Pharaoh.

In many ways, Joseph's story reveals the central challenge of psychological development, and that is the willingness of the ego to submit to the Self, or God. It is the necessity of the ego to give up its former identification with the Self. Edward Edinger speaks of this in his treatment of the story of Joseph. The robe that Joseph loses, his robe of distinction, is symbolic of the Self. "It is the garment of the Self and wearing it carelessly or unconsciously signifies ego-Self identity. For that reason Joseph must be stripped of it."[1]

This can be seen when the perfectionism (evidence of the ego's striving to be like God) revealed in the portraits of Candace and Karen gave way to humility—when both came to an acceptance of themselves as human, flawed individuals. In Joan's story, her ego was forced to give up its determination to deny the truth in order to keep a relationship. As a result, Joan is willing to live more authentically, even if it means giving up a relationship that is important to her.

For Joan, learning to live out her faith so that her beliefs were integrated with her behavior is what Candace referred to as praxis. It is an authentic way of living. And it seems that this is the most significant outgrowth of the transformation these women have experienced. For most, the goal of wanting to be liked has given way to a desire to act out of personal integrity.

1. What beliefs, ideas, or assumptions have you had to let go during your time of grief? Which of these was the most painful? What have you gained as a result of letting go? Write your answers in your journal.

2. Revisit the story of Joseph in Genesis chapters 37–45. Jungian analyst Edward Edinger describes Joseph's coat as a symbol of the perfectionism and self-aggrandizement that Joseph needed to be stripped of. Recall our discussion of the idea of humility. How has your experience of divorce humbled you? How has this changed the way you relate to others? To yourself?

CHAPTER NINE

What Went Wrong with My Marriage?

During a workshop exercise, my husband
Boasted how healthy he was and how
Together he was and I remember thinking,
That's not true. That's just not true!
—Joan

How will you come to understand?
Search. Seek and you will find.
—Brother Roger of Taizé

One of the most common questions at the end of a marriage is, "What went wrong?" As with any tragic event, we seek to understand how such a thing could have happened. What did I miss? What could I have done differently? And, perhaps most importantly: How can I prevent this from happening again?

This searching is part of what propels us forward in life in general, and our spiritual journeys in particular. In the early days, Christianity was called "The Way," and Jesus referred to himself as a road or path. Thus, as we envision the journey through the grief of divorce as an opportunity for spiritual formation, it makes sense to ponder some of the questions regarding the end of your marriage.

As you know from your own experience, people begin their marriages with high hopes for a lifetime of love and companionship. The wedding ceremony is a declaration to family and community that this is the person with whom you plan to spend the rest of your life.

For Christians, marriage is a sacrament. It is a symbol the Bible uses to describe the relationship of Jesus to the church, the "bride of Christ." So, in addition to declaring one's love and commitment before family and community, Christians stand before God vowing to "honor and cherish, till death do us part." Thus for Christians, divorce and the marital difficulties that preceded it are all the more challenging.

This is further compounded by the implication that divorce (and other tragedies) can be prevented if you do the right things. To that end, most churches require some kind of formal preparation prior to being married. This may include a series of classes, pastoral counseling, and assessments. In addition, there are the Bible studies, retreats, workshops, and seminars devoted to the topic of marriage.

But an unintended consequence of these activities is that they foster an unconscious bargain with God: "If I do (premarital counseling, go to church, pray, read my Bible, participate in marriage retreats, etc.), then God will keep me from getting divorced." As the individuals I interviewed for this book—and countless others—have discovered, you can do all these things and still end up divorced. So when divorce does happen despite all your best efforts, it can leave you confused and disoriented. "I did everything I was supposed to do. How could this happen?"

This is an important question because the answers will assist you in fully grieving the loss of your marriage and learning the lessons that grief has to teach. The short answer is that, as God made very clear to Job, His ways are mysterious. Life brings to everyone a measure of suffering. Jesus did not promise a life without suffering—only that He would be with us through the pain.

But to recognize the ultimate mystery of God's ways does not absolve us of the responsibility for finding answers. Much like Jacob wrestled with God, crying out for a blessing, so we too can wrestle with the questions of divorce. And perhaps, like Jacob, we too will be blessed, even if we walk away from the experience with a limp.

The most frequent misunderstandings about the causes of divorce

Beyond seeing divorce as one of the prices we pay for living in a fallen world, there are some common factors that contribute to chronic marital conflict, the knowledge of which can help prevent another divorce.

First, let's examine some of the most common reasons people give for their divorce. "I married the wrong person" is probably the most frequent explanation given. The problem with this assumption is that divorce statistics on second marriages don't bear this out. If someone married the wrong person the first time, it stands to reason that they would pick the right person the second time around. Thus you would expect second marriages to have a lower divorce rate than first marriages. Instead, the opposite is the case; second marriages divorce at a rate of 75%!

What people usually discover in their second marriages is that the same issues arise, perhaps in a different form, and often more quickly than in the first marriage. When you combine this with the pressures and challenges of dealing with ex-spouses, custody and child support issues, and stepchildren, you can see why the divorce rate among second marriages is so high.

Another common reason cited is, "We just grew apart." This is a little closer to the truth but not in ways one might think. Of course you grew and changed, but that was not the problem. The real issue is how each of you responded to the impetus to grow and change. As David Schnarch explains, marriage brings every couple to what he calls "emotional gridlock."[1] This means that each person has come to the end of their pretense with one another, the end of what they already know how to do to maintain emotional harmony, and it is at this point that the real work of marriage begins.

Emotional gridlock is well-depicted in the Dr. Seuss story of the Zax, in which two individuals who walk along the "Prairie of Prax" eventually meet and arrive at an impasse. Neither one of them will move to the left or the right in order to the let other pass. Instead, they stand facing each other in stubborn determination not to alter their course. They stand through the seasons—the rain, the snow. Finally a freeway overpass is built around the two Zax and they stand to this day "unbudged in their tracks."[2]

This is what emotional gridlock can be like. Many, if not most people, will eventually resolve emotional gridlock by divorcing. The problem with this solution is that eventually each will replicate this gridlock with another individual.

Another reason that is often given for divorce is that the ex-spouse was the problem. "My ex-wife or my ex-husband was (an alcoholic, an adulterer, a drug addict, emotionally or physically abusive, has a personality disorder, etc.)." While this may be true, it begs the question: What made you decide to marry such a person? This is not to "blame the victim" but rather to empower you not to make such a decision again.

Often when I ask this question of clients, they will say something like "He or she was not like that when we met." While I know that marriage does change the nature of a relationship, it is also usually the case that these behaviors felt "familiar" and thus were not noticed. In other words, this person fit with the family system.

Conversely, other people blame themselves for their divorce. "I should have (been a better partner, been more thoughtful, been more submissive, etc.)." I usually tell my clients that the most they should accept is half of the responsibility for the end of their marriage. Each partner had choices they could have made to change themselves within the relationship. Learning what your marriage was asking you to change about yourself, and then working to make those changes now, will help you in all your relationships now and in the future.

As you can see, there are a number of reasons that people think contributed to the end of their marriages. But such is not the case. The truth lies in the inability to resolve an emotional impasse. This chapter will examine the most common impasses that manifest themselves in marriage. Understanding these dynamics will help you learn the lessons of divorce, move toward changing your part in the patterns, and thus lay the groundwork for better relationships in the future.

Conflict/Cutoff: The teeter-totter experience

We have all had the déjà vu experience of recurring arguments that rehash the same issues over and over again. And, even when the argument is a new one, we can experience the same kind of overwhelming discouragement and frustration. We are usually very focused on the other person, trying to make sure that he or she "gets it." "If only he understood." "If only she would see my point of view." "Why is he/she so stubborn?"

Sometimes, in our frustration, we get "bigger"—speak more loudly, use more volatile language—as though this might get through to the other person. During these times, our physiology begins to take over and we are literally incapable of thinking clearly, or even really thinking at all! This explains why we can have an especially intense argument and not remember the details later on.

What usually follows is some kind of emotional or physical cutoff. Each partner retreats, feeling wounded and misunderstood, and things cool down a bit. Because the emotional intensity of these arguments is so painful, most people choose to avoid the topic. *Why bring that up again? I know what will happen,* they think; as a result, the issue remains unaddressed. At some point, though, the situation occurs again, and another painful argument ensues.

Many couples live on the cycle of conflict/cutoff for years. This may have been the case for you in your marriage. Eventually the constant tension and the wear and tear of years of conflict take their toll, and most couples who experience a long-term pattern of conflict/cutoff will divorce. This pattern, however, is not limited to marriages. It occurs between parents and children, brothers and sisters, aunts, uncles and cousins. So even though you are no longer married, it is important to learn how to change your part in this pattern. Let's begin with examining how our physiology is involved.

Fight, Flight or Freeze: Understanding the physiology of anger

The human body is an amazing creation; every moment of your life, systems are working to protect you from all types of threats both physical and emotional. One of these defense systems involves the limbic area of the brain, which is responsible for sending out an alarm when you are threatened. It does this so efficiently and quickly that it bypasses the neocortex (responsible for thought and judgment) before it is able to assess the possible consequences of your actions.

One reason your brain is wired this way is because thinking requires a lot of energy, and when you are sufficiently threatened, you need all your resources to defend yourself by fighting or fleeing. As a result, your thinking processes shut down and your body goes into overdrive. Your muscles tense; your heart rate increases; your blood pressure rises; adrenaline pours through your body; your attention narrows to include only the target of your anger. This is life-saving if you're getting out of the way of a fast-moving car, but it can be relationship-destroying when you are involved in an argument with someone you love.

All is not lost, however, because it is possible to manage this reaction. To do so, though, means that you must understand and respect the physiology of anger and intervene early enough in the process. You want to make full use of your cognitive functioning. When you feel yourself becoming defensive, this is a signal that, unless you change something, the fight-or-flight process will begin.

Usually, people ignore the early warning signs within themselves as well as others and continue to stay in an argument long past the point of no return. As the argument progresses, both parties become more and more focused on the other, their physiology becomes more and more anxiously aroused, and soon they are hurling statements at one another that they wouldn't say to their worst enemies. Sometimes these exchanges even move beyond verbal assaults and one or both parties may resort to physical attacks.

You may be thinking, *I never get angry, so this can't be my problem.* Because anger is an innate emotional response, this means that you either suppress your anger or deny it altogether. An example of this came from a male client who used tell me, rather proudly, "I just take the hit." His efforts to suppress his anger, however, merely resulted in escalating that of his wife. The more he stonewalled, the louder she became until at some point she actually did get a reaction, though not a very pleasant one.

A better alternative would have been for him to calmly respond to his wife's escalating anger by telling her that he was interested in hearing what she had to say but that her shouting made it impossible to do so. If she wasn't willing to lower her voice, he could explain that he would be interested in discussing her concerns later and calmly leave the room.

In order to clear his mind, he could get involved in a physical activity or some other engaging pursuit, and he could also invite his wife to join him. Later on, he could arrange to continue the discussion with his wife. This is in fact what I suggested.

"But she'll just follow me out of the room," he explained. "What do I do then?" I recommended that he tell her that while he did want to listen to her, emotions were running too high and this prevented him from doing so. In this case, the client did just that and it proved helpful to them both.

If you are thinking, *That's impossible!* you're partially correct. It is impossible if you wait too long. It is also impossible if you are firmly convinced that the other person is the problem. "If he wouldn't yell at every little thing, I wouldn't get so angry" or "If she would stop nagging me, I wouldn't have to yell at her to stop." This is true, but then you're dependent on what the other person decides to do. Instead, by changing yourself in these habitual interactions, you will be empowering yourself to create the life you want.

One of my clients experienced this with her ex-husband in the early days of their divorce. He threatened her with suing for complete custody, asking for an evaluation by the courts of her competency as a mother, etc. She and I reviewed her part in this escalation. It soon became evident that she found it extremely difficult to stop participating in arguments with him. If he texted her a nasty message on her cell phone, she would text him a similar one back. Or she would become defensive and try to get him to be reasonable. "He needs to understand…" was a common refrain. The problem was that any kind of engagement with her ex-husband only increased the emotional intensity.

My client worked hard to change this pattern—one that had actually started in her childhood when she was the "referee" between her arguing parents. Once she started to respond to the factual part of the email or text message and ignored the "hook" to engage in another argument, things calmed down dramatically. Keep in mind that she was not to blame for the emotional intensity—he was just as responsible as she was. But she learned that she could change her part in maintaining this pattern and that went a long way toward creating a more peaceful life for her and her children.

Emotional Allergy: The result of chronic relational intensity

When a couple regularly engages in hurtful behaviors over a long period of time, they become more and more sensitized to the other. My husband, Ron, calls this an "emotional allergy." In the same way a physical allergy automatically sets off a series of responses to an allergen, an emotional allergy results in heightened emotional arousal, a hyper-alert state that causes each partner to become uncomfortable when in the presence of the other. Couples who divorce are usually very uncomfortable and anxious around each other. One client explained, "The minute I see one of his emails, I can feel myself tense up." You can see that it would not take much to begin the process of fight or flight—a raised eyebrow, a sigh, a look of exasperation—and off they go to the races.

Changing your part in the conflict/cutoff pattern

So what can you do to change your part in this pattern? To begin with, you'll need to become much more aware of your physical and emotional responses. You'll need to take the focus off your ex-spouse and redirect it to yourself. This would mean that you become aware of your first feeling of defensiveness or hurt. You become aware of the rise in your blood pressure and the increasing tension in your muscles that signal the start of the fight-or-flight process. And when you do, you change your habitual response. This might mean that you disengage temporarily from the discussion—even if you don't want to or even if your ex-spouse doesn't want you to.

You'll want to do this, however, without creating more damage. This means that you wouldn't hurl a final parting shot as you leave, or slam a door in his face, or with screeching tires, drive off to the nearest bar in order to "show her." You would disengage by explaining, "This isn't working for me. I'm feeling defensive. I'm not able to listen to you right now."

Notice that this statement is about you, not your ex-spouse. It is not, "You better stop yelling or I'm going to walk out on you," but rather, "This is what I'm going to do to manage myself." As I tell my clients, "Walk the talk! If you say it isn't okay to yell, you need to back that up with a behavior. You need to stop yelling and you need to do something when your ex starts yelling at you." Keep in mind that the "doing" should be in keeping with your values and ideals.

Will your ex-spouse rejoice with your newfound awareness of your limitations? Probably not. Typically he or she will try to get you to stay in the argument. Perhaps he will continue to make nasty comments. Or perhaps she will cast aspersions on your manhood, saying that a real man would not walk away from a fight. Thus, you would do well to prepare to stick to your position by thinking through the possible scenarios when you say, "I'm finished for now. I want to get back to this later, but I'm not able to listen to you right now."

Once you have done this, have calmed down, and are able to think more clearly, you will then want to check in with your ex-spouse and arrange to resume the discussion. This can be the most difficult part of changing your part in this pattern. *Why would I want to do that?* you might be thinking. *We'll only get into another argument.*

There are several reasons for reengaging the topic. First, the reason for the argument will not go away, and if it was important enough to argue about, that should be a signal that something needs to be addressed. Second, resuming discussion when things are calm and you can be thoughtful will increase your chances of successfully resolving the conflict. Third, bringing up the topic again will mean that you have changed your typical response. You do this by letting your ex know that you would like to continue the discussion. This would also include negotiating for a good time to talk and any other parameters—perhaps a time limit—in order to regulate emotional intensity. This is how you take care of yourself in the long run.

Playing hide and seek: Pursuer/distancer dynamics

Another common relationship pattern is that of pursuer/distancer. This is not necessarily a problem unless the pattern becomes inflexible and polarized. You may be a pursuer in one relationship and a distancer in another. Likewise, you may be a pursuer in one area of your relationship and a distancer in another. For instance, a man may be a pursuer in the sexual aspect of a marriage while he is a distancer in terms of emotional relatedness. Each person in this pattern or dance plays an important role in maintaining the degree of distance that each is comfortable with in a relationship.

Generally, the pursuer will have more of an affinity for relationship time and be more comfortable with expressing personal feelings and thoughts. He or she may also be relatively non-selective in self-disclosure. The distancer, on the other hand, will have an affinity for alone time, or activity time. He or she may tend to avoid expressing personal feelings and thoughts and be relatively overly selective in disclosure. The pursuer narrows the distance and maintains a connection. The distancer ensures that the relationship does not become too volatile and that boundaries are respected.

When these roles become rigid and inflexible, the marriage can become conflicted. The pursuer will move toward the distancer; as she does, the distancer will shift away. In response, the pursuer pursues more intensely and the distancer responds in kind. Eventually, the pursuer will tire of the pursuit and move away in a reactive distance, at which point the distancer will tentatively move toward the pursuer.

However, once the pursuer moves toward the partner again, the distancer quickly backs off. Finally the pursuer begins to attack the distancer (a form of pursuit, albeit an unpleasant one) who will defend himself, often resorting to attacking as well. Over time, the couple can remain at a fixed distance in a relationship that is characterized by antagonism and resentment.

The problem is not the behavior of the pursuer or distancer, but rather the *focus of attention*. As long as they are anxiously focused on each other, nothing will change. Thus keeping the focus on oneself, on what one can do and will do based on principles and values, will change the dynamics of the relationship.

Though you are now divorced, this dynamic may continue to play out in your relationship with your ex. If you were the pursuer in the marriage, you may still find yourself pursuing your ex-spouse, only now it is to arrange the time to drop off the kids or the schedule for the coming week. Or, conversely, you could play the role of the distancer. Perhaps you have convinced yourself that you and your children would be better off without your spouse and try your hardest to put as much distance as possible between your ex-spouse and yourself and your children.

Changing your part in the pursuer/distancer pattern

The best way to change yourself within this dynamic is to allow your values—rather than your emotions—to guide your behaviors. Only you will be able to really judge when this is the case.

An example of this occurred recently with a client who had played the part of pursuer in her marriage to a husband who distanced emotionally. In this instance, her now ex-husband sent her an email asking if he could take the children on a trip that would require them to miss about a week of school. He had waited until just a few days before to ask my client, who in the past would have been frustrated and angry with him for "forcing her" to make a decision at the last minute. But this time, she told him she would need to think about it and get back to him.

She reviewed her values—one of which is for her children to spend time with their father, regardless of what she may think about him as a husband—and decided that she would agree to this if he made the arrangements with the children's school and teachers. Emails went back and forth as he continued to negotiate changes in the arrangements, but she was able to remain factual and avoid responding out of anger or frustration (at least in the emails to him!).

This was an important learning experience for her because in the past she might have just capitulated (making all of the arrangements as well!) or rejected the idea outright because she was tired of feeling taken advantage of. Either of those responses would have been an emotional, knee-jerk reaction. She used this opportunity to grow herself with her ex-husband and felt empowered as a result.

Loading and off-loading: The overfunctioner/ underfunctioner dynamic

"If I don't do it, nobody else will!" is the familiar cry of the overfunctioner and a hallmark of the third relational dynamic: the overfunctioner/ underfunctioner pattern. A common example of this can be seen in the relationship between a parent and a child in which the parent continues to overfunction for the child well into adulthood. I saw this over and over again when I worked in chemical dependency treatment facilities where parents were paying for the adult child's fifth, tenth, or even twentieth treatment program. This is a dramatic example, but it illustrates the way in which individuals can become stuck in a pattern that is obviously problematic for all concerned.

In marriages, individuals often overfunction in different areas. The husband may overfunction in the financial realm, perhaps serving as the sole breadwinner for the family; the wife may overfunction in the area of parenting, partly in response to the husband's need to earn a living. This does not need to be a problem but can easily descend into one if the individuals becomes polarized in their roles. Just as with all inflexible patterns, the overfunctioner/ underfunctioner dynamic is the result of a habitual (usually unconscious) anxious response.

Thus in the above example the wife may feel overburdened and complain that her husband does not help out enough with the kids but then criticize his parenting. Likewise, a husband may complain that he is burdened with responsibility for household chores but become upset when his wife pays a handyman to finish up some of the ongoing projects.

It is also interesting to note that wives who believed their husbands were incapable of caring for their children become much more trusting of them after a divorce. Now, with joint custody, the fathers care for the children fifty percent of the time, and many men have noted that they became better fathers after their divorce. Somehow being married decreased their abilities to think clearly about the types of fathers they wanted to be; instead, they reacted to their wives' increased anxiety (as in "you're not doing it right!").

Likewise, women who underfunctioned in the area of finances often become much more conscientious about money management once they're responsible for providing for their livelihood. The intensity of the marital relationship resulted in an inability to think clearly in this area of their lives.

Changing your part in the overfunctioner/ underfunctioner pattern

Though the overfunctioner usually is the most motivated to change, whether you are an overfunctioner or underfunctioner, you will want work to change your habitual responses. Once again, you will want to allow your principles and values— rather than your emotions—to guide you.

For instance, if you believe your ex-spouse is not spending enough time with the children, instead of reacting out of frustration, wait until you are calm and can be curious about what your ex-spouse is thinking. Ask him what he thinks his role as a parent should be. How much time does she think is enough time to spend with the children every week? What prevents him from setting limits with the kids? What can you do to help make this happen?

While you can share your observations, do so as factually as you can. This means without the editorializing or finger-pointing that so often accompanies these types of discussions. "You are acting like a babysitter!" and "When are you going to start acting like a father?" are not going to assist you in having a thoughtful discussion. Remember, you are not your ex-spouse's teacher! The idea is change yourself, not your ex-spouse.

Guidelines for change

1. Observe yourself. Before you can begin to change, you need to know what your typical reactions are to your ex-spouse. Set aside one week for establishing a baseline. What happens to you when

you see him? What changes in you when she calls? Do you feel your heart start to race? Do you find it difficult to think clearly? Is anger your first reaction to him—regardless of the circumstances?

2. Learn to lower your reactivity. Once you know how you tend to react, practice restoring yourself by focusing on your reactions and settling yourself down. Start out with a relatively easy task and then work up to a more challenging discussion. Perhaps you can start by opening up an email from your ex-spouse, taking some deep breaths, and highlight the factual aspects of the email while ignoring those that might "hook" you into a fight.

3. Respond factually. Instead of responding in kind to an emotional email or text, respond as though they made a request that was factual. For example, if the email says, "You are so inconsiderate! Why can't you just drop the kids off on time for once! I am tired of waiting for you all the time. If you were …," you could respond by saying, "You'd like the kids dropped off on time. What time did you have in mind?" I realize that this seems impossible. Your ex is likely to be very good at touching on sensitive issues. The tendency is to want to "teach" the other person that they can't get away with talking to us like that! The truth is, you will not teach your ex-spouse anything and only participate in another argument.

4. Pray! Changing yourself in an intense relationship is a challenging undertaking to say the least! Don't rely on your own strength to follow through on these recommendations. Remember that when Jesus said that for God nothing is impossible, He was talking about these types of challenges. What seems impossible for you is not if you turn to the source of all peace and strength.

5. Trust the process. At first, you may see an escalation in attempts to get you to react the way you normally would. This is normal and

expected. Continue to hold onto your new position and eventually this will be the new normal.

6. Work on other relationships. Your ex-spouse is not the only challenging relationship in your life. Identify others with whom you can practice these ideas—your mother, father, sister, brother, children, etc. These all offer you opportunities to work to change yourself.

7. Find a licensed counselor to assist you. Growing yourself can be difficult at times, and it can be very challenging to try to do this on your own. Much like trying to see yourself without a mirror, trying to make significant changes in your life without a trained, licensed counselor can be very hard. A good counselor should be able to assist you within six to ten sessions in seeing positive results. You'll find some suggestions for finding a qualified counselor in the back of this book.

Working to change yourself with your ex-spouse, as well as other important people in your life, will help to redeem the pain and suffering of divorce. It is the underpinning to a transformed life, one that is characterized by more fulfilling relationships and a deeper relationship with God. This can be seen in our next chapter featuring Jeanne's story of divorce and transformation.

1. Which of the patterns of relationship dynamics do you identify with the most strongly? Select a relationship in which you are still playing your usual part in the pattern. Next, write a brief description of a recent example and then apply the steps to change listed above. Practice making a change in this relationship this week. Write about your experiences in your journal.

2. Read 1 Corinthians 14:20–40. What are some childish behaviors you would like to set aside? How do these show up in the above

listed relationship patterns? Ask God to help you practice changing your part in these patterns, regardless of the behaviors of the
other person.

3. Set aside some time to draw a timeline of your spiritual journey.
   Do this by taking a piece of paper (or perhaps taping several
   together) and drawing a line, noting each significant incident
   and the age at which it occurred. You might recall times of God's
   absence, of confusion and pain, as well as those in which you felt
   God's presence most fully. Ask yourself, *Where do I see God's
   hand in my life now that I am looking back?* You can further illus-
   trate your timeline if you want with photographs, pictures from
   magazines, or your own illustrations.

CHAPTER TEN

An Amazing Adventure (Jeanne's Story)

Like Magellan; let us find our islands
To die in, far from home, from anywhere
Familiar. Let us risk the wildest places,
Lest we go down in comfort and despair.

—Mary Oliver
New and Selected Poems

I really haven't thought about my marriage in a long time, but its ending was truly the beginning of an incredible adventure. I was married right out of high school to a much older man—he admitted to 40, though he could have been older than that. He was very youthful and a lot of fun, so the age difference didn't really matter much to me. He was really interested in the world at large, and that made him an interesting person to be with. At the time, my ideas about a good marriage were not well-formed, so I thought our marriage was pretty good. He treated me well; he constantly reinforced his love for me when he bought me flowers and gifts, took me out to dinner, and verbally expressed how much he appreciated having someone like me in his life.

So I do believe that in his own way he loved me. However, looking back now, I can see that there was quite a bit of distance. He was gone a lot with his work and that was a problem for me. I wanted more emotional intimacy and I remember bringing that need to him, but I wouldn't say I was miserable. In fact, now that I know myself better, I realize that I'm the type of person who can spend time alone and who needs space, so, in many ways, the marriage worked for me.

Still, something was missing in the marriage and in my life, and I remember praying about it. I remember I was on my knees one day and said, "Lord, something is not right about this marriage and I don't know what it is. You've got to make things the way You want them to be. I just want You to be Lord of my life." And the thought came very clearly to me, *What if it means your marriage?* This struck me as a really unexpected question to come to mind when praying. I recall telling God I wanted His will for my life.

Right after that I found out that my husband had been having an affair with one of my friends. I think on some level I must have known, but I didn't consciously realize it. I was pretty well devastated when I found out; his attitude and the way he admitted it made it even harder. He said things like, "I don't love you anymore; and I'm not in love with you." So it was like night and day. One minute he was telling me how much he cherished me and the next he said he didn't. I remember thinking, *What is reality here?* I had this entire life that I thought was one way and it was actually something else. Talk about deception!

I really identified with Joseph's plight of rejection by his family. I held onto Joseph's statement. You meant it for evil, but God meant it for good. My faith in God was really strengthened after that; I learned I could run to Him for comfort. This was really important to me because for two years my husband was in and out of the marriage. I'd forgive him and take him back, and then he'd do it again. Finally I couldn't endure the pain anymore and we separated.

My ex-husband never paid child support. In fact, he never contacted my daughter again. He actually went to Hawaii with the woman he had the affair with on a boat we owned. It was really hard. It was hard to see my child suffering, especially when I felt somewhat responsible for having married the guy against the advice of family and friends. Also, he had been my first love—the only man I had ever been with, so the loss was incredible.

I had been praying that if God wanted us together, He would work a miracle, but I began to see that at least financially, I needed to do something. It was the late 1970s and my husband left with all but $10,000 of the $100,000 equity we had from the sale of our house and the furniture. I was in pretty desperate emotional and financial straits as a young mother with a seven-year-old daughter and without a college education.

I really didn't believe in divorce and, in fact, wasn't going to get one. But friends from church told me, "Jeanne, you've got to get a divorce. He's left. He won't give up doing what he's been doing."

By that time I had started to work in real estate, and though I did well financially, it was difficult to spend quality time with my daughter because of the demands of open houses on the weekends and purchase offers in the evenings. I also felt a deep sense of guilt and responsibility toward my child. She was really devastated by the departure of her father since they had been unbelievably close. It was rough because I was emotionally in such turmoil, but I knew I needed to help her through her grief and pain. In light of that, I decided that I would start an in-home business because I would be able to schedule my time in such a way that I could be home with her when she was home.

For that first year after I started the business, we were essentially homeless because I didn't have enough income to pay rent. So we ended up house-sitting for various people in our church while they went on vacation. People were really generous; they'd leave the refrigerator full of food. I don't know how we made it during those lean years except for God. During this time I discovered and held onto Scripture that has since guided my life, Isaiah 54:4–7 (AMP), which says: "Fear not, for you shall not be ashamed; neither be confounded and depressed, for you shall not be put to shame. For you shall forget the shame of your youth, and you shall not seriously remember the reproach of your widowhood any more. For your Maker is your Husband—the Lord of hosts is His name—and the Holy One of Israel is your Redeemer; the God of the whole earth He is called. For the Lord has called you like a woman forsaken, grieved in spirit, and heartsore—even a wife wooed and won in youth, when she is later refused and scorned, says your God. For a brief moment I forsook you, but with great compassion and mercy I will gather you to Me again."

I've seen this promise become a reality in my life over and over again.

Shortly after that, I met a Christian man and we dated for about 13 months. I think that if I had been a healthier person, I would have known to wait, but I was so used to being married, and the concept of being dependent on a man was so well-formed in me, that I kind of just responded to him on the rebound. I mean, he was tall, dark, good-looking, and we got along great.

At the time, we were in our twenties, but we had had such different life experiences. I had been married already and had a child, and he wasn't sure if that was what he wanted in his life. I thought this new relationship was an answer to prayer, but then I heard the Lord so clearly say, "If you think this is worth waiting for, wait until you see what I am going to do." I resisted that because I had already made up my mind that if he asked, I was inclined to marry him.

While he was praying about marriage to me during that time, he met another woman and believed she was the one that God meant for him. I was really hurt and my daughter was once again crushed; she really thought this guy would be her new dad! I decided right then and there: Dating would have to go on the back burner of my life until she was launched into the world. As much as was in my power, I would refrain from anything that would cause her further pain as a result of my actions.

By this time, I had my own place, which I shared with a roommate, so things were improving financially. I had taken an entry-level government job, and though I was told I was really overqualified for that position, I was promised a promotion as soon as an opening was available. Things were really tight financially for a long time. I used to make a chicken last a whole week! We laugh about it now, but it was tough at the time.

I was considering a promotion at work that would require my commuting quite a distance from my home. Then I had this dream in which a faceless man was telling me, "You don't want to travel all the way to Huntington Beach for a promotion. You want a promotion here at home." And I said, "But there are no promotions here at home." And he said, "Wait and see."

Again, like Joseph, I really believed in God's promises through dreams. Shortly after that dream, I was recruited in an elevator, of all places, for a position as a Special Agent with another government agency. Later I learned the position included a government car and an opportunity to write reports at my home.

For a long time, I didn't know what God meant when He said, "Wait 'til you see what I'm going to do." But after this I began to suspect that maybe it was a promise for my career. I thought, *Well, God's not giving me a husband, but he's given me a great career to put my energy into and an exciting life.*

One day I was at Monarch Beach doing an investigation at a home that had a gorgeous ocean view. And I realized that I was envying this guy his ocean view! I really felt that I would never be in a position to have an ocean-view home.

That same evening, my landlord gave my roommate and me 30 days notice. So I thought, *Great. Now I have to move in 30 days and I'm not prepared to do this.* Well, it turned out that this was the open door for me to find the place I had scarcely dared to hope for—a townhouse with an ocean view. The Lord worked it out for me to become a homeowner!

Here's the icing on the cake: It's on the same street that the guy I almost married used to live. Previously, every time I drove by, I'd kind of get this sick feeling inside because it had been such a disappointment. Now, God has given me a joy in this very place of one of my greatest disappointments. God has been such an incredible provider for me. It's just been unbelievable.

Just before I moved into my townhouse, I had a dream that I was in a field and there were huge plants that towered over my head. Then I came to this opening and there was a waterfall. I jumped into it and this guy jumped in with me. We ended up in a beautiful pool and we were floating in the water. He had his arm around me and he was stroking my hair, which had a beautiful flower in it. I felt this overwhelming sense of love, like I'd never had before. The sense of love was so powerful I awoke and sat up in bed. It was so intense and so real.

About three years later, I was sent to Hawaii on a special assignment. When I got there, I was informed my job as a Special Agent in California was downsizing and I had seven days to decide what I wanted to do. They gave me several options, one of which was a job in Hawaii. I remembered the dream I had about the waterfall and wondered if this was what God was communicating to me in that dream. As a result, I took that position, and I worked in Hawaii for two wonderful years. Shortly thereafter, I was offered a promotion with the Department of Justice and relocated back to southern California.

I look back over the past several years and just marvel; I have had the most incredible experiences. I was in Africa for two months last year doing refugee resettlement for family reunification as part of my new job. There are still people living in some parts of Africa just like they have since biblical times.

I've traveled to places throughout the world. I recently returned from a special assignment in Rome, Italy. World travel has made me a much more open person, I think. It has widened my perspective. I no longer think that the culture we live in is the only one that is correct; there are many cultures where things are done differently. The Christian culture here is really a sub-culture of American culture, and unfortunately can be really narrow and unaccepting. Jesus was not like this.

I no longer think I know how God should work in someone's life. What can I tell you? I have a very good friend at work that has a different lifestyle, but I told him, "I don't have all the answers. All I know is that God has put this love in my heart for you as a person." I'm not trying to rescue him or have him change his lifestyle—I just pray for him in hope he finds God's love. I have to say, in many ways I have a better friendship with him than I do with some of the men at church. He's honest and kind and he cares about people.

I've also discovered that I have a heart for women's issues. I was the women's program manager at work for two years, and I'm very concerned about the role of women, in and out of the church. The church that I'm comfortable with is a church that allows a woman to be a whole person. My idea of submission at this point is cooperation—mutual respect, partnership. This is a little different than what is taught in some churches.

Given the life experience that I've had, I don't see myself attached to someone who would expect me to turn over my paycheck and have him dole out the money. I know there are some individuals in leadership in the Christian church that really think that's the biblical way, but I disagree. I don't think that is what the Word teaches about the marital relationship. I see a lot of women in our church who are dealing with some big issues, like emotional and physical abuse, which is not really addressed in some church groups. That concerns me.

My experience since my divorce has really made me less dependent on men and more dependent on God. It's made me focus on my own happiness, and what would be a fulfilling use of my talents and abilities. Before my divorce, my belief was that the wife's job was to make the husband happy; a good wife does everything for her husband. But now I want a man who is self-sufficient enough to be responsible for his own happiness. So far I haven't met anyone like that, so it may be that God's suggestion of waiting to see what He was going to do for me was not a promise that included remarriage.

I think that my willingness to open myself up to the opportunities that have presented themselves in my life has enabled me to have a life that I never dreamed possible. God opened the doors for me and I stepped through them—even though at times, I had very little understanding of what His purpose was. It's just amazing to me all that God has given me.

REFLECTION

As with any significant loss, divorce thrusts people into the unknown. All of the hopes and dreams, as well as the day-to-day reality of a person's life, are gone. Consequently, the person is faced with creating a new life out of the wreckage of the old. To venture forth into uncharted territory takes a great deal of courage. For some people, there are at least some vestiges of the old life to bring with them. They may remain in the same house, continue to work at the same jobs, and if they are parents, they will continue to maintain some kind of contact with their former spouse.

But such was not the case for Jeanne. Her divorce literally left her homeless. Her husband ceased all forms of contact with her. She had no job to fall back on. So, except for her daughter, there was little left of her old life. What she did have was a strong faith and the wisdom of her dreams to guide her.

Though in modern times dreams are seldom understood as a means of communication with God, such was not the case in times past. As John Sanford points out, "It is clear that in the Book of Genesis dreams were regarded as manifestations of divine intention, as one of God's ways of communicating with people."[1] This is certainly the way Jeanne experienced her dreams; this, in turn, underscored much of her confidence in moving forward despite the uncertainties that lay before her.

What Jeanne's experience shows is that out of the pain and suffering that comes with loss can come a new relationship with God and with oneself. Jeanne's willingness to listen to the messages of her dreams enabled her to experience life in a new way. The same can be said for the other women in this book; their willingness to encounter the unknown about themselves and God opened them up to a new way of thinking about themselves and others. Each person in this book relates a profound change in her relationships, both with herself and with others.

This is a hallmark of what Carl Jung identified as the process of individuation, which he saw as a journey toward wholeness. Individuation involves incorporating previously disowned aspects of oneself, which are largely unconscious, into the conscious attitude of the individual. That which we know about our own selves is fairly limited. To paraphrase Jesus, we can see the speck in the eyes of others far easier than the log that is in our own. In order to know ourselves, to become more fully who God created us to be, we need to be willing to accept feedback about ourselves from others (including ex-spouses!) and from different sources, including that of our dreams, which Sanford calls "God's forgotten language."[2]

A basic requirement for this process, though, is the development of a strong ego. Sanford describes a strong ego as "a conscious personality capable of exerting itself effectively in life." The irony is that while we are given the task of developing a strong ego during the first half of our adulthood, we will then be called to give it up in service of God's will. As Sanford explains, "Only a person with a strong ego can give up that ego; we cannot give to God what we do not possess."[3]

This paradoxical notion lies at the heart of what Jung means by individuation because ultimately, a relationship with God will call for a willingness on the part of the ego, or the conscious attitude, to renounce itself. When we are young and our ego is developing, we are usually unaware that there is anything greater than us at work in our lives. For most people, the ego is the sum total of the psychological universe.

As a person develops and encounters evidence to the contrary, divorce being one example, a greater appreciation develops for the limitation of the ego. In other words, we learn that despite our best efforts, events are frequently out of our control. Often there have been several instances where the person experiences events unfolding outside of his or her own conscious control, yet, at the same time, revealing a greater purpose to the individual's existence. To renounce one's conscious desires is not a false martyrdom, which is often a cheap facsimile of this experience, but rather a means by which the person's existence becomes tied into something greater, into the transcendent God.

This is what Jeanne experienced in her life. A sense that something greater than her was working in her life, revealing things and opening doors to experiences that her conscious attitude would never have imagined.

1. John Sanford, in *Dreams: God's Forgotten Language*, reminds us that God can and does reveal Himself in our dreams. "All of us dream," he writes, "and our dreams always have a meaningful message."[4] Take a few minutes to recall a recent dream. If you can't, make a point to remember a dream that you might have

tonight. Set our journal next to your bed and write down what you remember as you wake up. Write your dream in the present tense: "I am in a large house that is not my own." Once you have written the dream in your journal, review it and circle any words that have the most emotional content for you. Perhaps it might be the word "house." Next write some of your associations to those words— any thoughts or images that come to mind. For house it might be "home" or "dwelling" or "love and safety" or "drudgery." As you review your list of associations, see if you can't see a theme emerge. What might God be revealing to you about yourself or your life circumstances? For more assistance with this, read *Inner Work* by Robert Johnson.[5]

2. Read the story of Jacob wrestling with the angel in Genesis 32. As you do so, put yourself in Jacob's position. Imagine what it would be like to wrestle all night long. What might you feel? How does Jacob's story resonate with your life's journey thus far? How have you wrestled with God? What does it mean to "walk with a limp" as a result?

CHAPTER ELEVEN

Your Ex-Spouse: Your Emotional Workout Partner

*Becoming more differentiated is probably
the most loving thing you can do in
your lifetime—for those you love
as well as yourself.*
—David Schnarch
Passionate Marriage

*That is how you have to be—
like the dead; beyond cursing
and praise, unaffected by the
opinions of others.*
—A desert father as quoted by Alan Jones
Soul Making

The journey through the grief of divorce takes you through many surprising twists and turns and through challenging encounters with new and unexpected truths. One of these is the fact that your exspouse can be an important resource in your personal, emotional, and spiritual growth. Though this is probably a jarring notion, it is in keeping with Jesus' exhortation to do good to those who seek to harm us, to hold the well-being of the other as valuable as our own. The Christian way is characterized by paradox—the infinite, omnipotent God who comes to earth as a tiny, helpless human infant; the man who must give up his life in order to save it; the woman who is asked to sit at Jesus' feet when there is work to be done.

From this perspective, it is possible to understand that someone who may be the most difficult person you know can be an instrument of your spiritual development. The truth is that sometimes we learn more from those who wound us than from those who give us comfort. Those experiences that are the most difficult have the potential for yielding the greatest rewards.

This is an understanding we tend to accept when it comes to physical exercise. Getting into good physical shape requires effort and some degree of suffering. It takes self-discipline to work out regularly because our natural inclination is to be sedentary—to expend the least amount of energy possible. But for those who push through this natural barrier, the rewards of exercising are worth the sacrifice of momentary pleasure. This, in turn, makes it easier to overcome the pull toward the comfy sofa and the TV and maintain a regular workout routine.

In much the same way, the desire for personal and spiritual growth is often impeded by our natural tendencies to stay within our emotional comfort zones—to respond to situations the way we always have in the past, the way our families have for generations, the way our culture and society says to respond. I think this is what Jesus meant when He spoke about the difference between the wide way and the narrow way. The wide way is smooth and easy, and there are a lot of people traveling that road; the narrow way is challenging, a bit rocky, and more difficult to traverse. But that is the road Jesus is on, the one He exhorts us to take because ultimately it is the way toward our highest good.

Changing yourself within the context of your relationship with your ex-spouse is taking the narrow way. Learning to respond differently to your ex-spouse than you have in the past, to respond in a way that is antithetical to the accepted view of others, will help you not only on a pragmatic level—fewer nasty arguments, easier co-parenting, emotional freedom—but perhaps most importantly, you will be actively participating in your psychological and spiritual development.

Differentiation: A psychological idea with spiritual implications

The term "differentiation" was first used in the context of human relationships by Dr. Murray Bowen, founder of Bowen Family Systems theory, and holds that the goal of emotional and psychological growth is to learn to be fully yourself—to think clearly and act on values and principles—while remaining in meaningful contact with members of your family.

Differentiation is a notion that is somewhat related to Carl Jung's idea of "individuation" in which the goal of psychological growth is to become a fully authentic and integrated self, aware of—but not driven by—unconscious forces.

But a significant difference in these two ideas lies in the soil from which they were created. Jung's idea of individuation is derived from philosophy, particularly that of Hegel, who held that transformation lies in the synthesis of two seemingly opposite forces ("thesis" and "antithesis"), and Kant, who argued that individuals are accountable for acting morally and ethically.

These two streams of thought are contained within the idea of individuation—a person's lifelong journey involves the reintegration of the unconscious, split-off aspects of one's self. In doing that, one is better able to see the log in one's own eye and become less focused on the speck in the eye of another.

In contrast, the concept of differentiation has its beginnings in the field of cellular biology. For instance, all of the cells in the leaf of an oak tree are connected, yet each is fully distinct. If they were not connected, there would be no leaf—just free-floating individual cells. However, if they were not distinct, the leaf would not exist either; there would only exist a clump of cells. As each cell divides and multiplies, the new cells remain in connection with the others even as each cell is separate. When applied to a family system, differentiation means learning to respond to intense emotional experiences differently than your family has done in the past, while maintaining regular and meaningful contact with its members.

Characteristics of a differentiated person

Someone who is differentiated has the ability to think clearly even in the wake of intense feelings, guided by values and principles rather than propelled by emotions. The person who is fully differentiated:

- has the courage to define self

- is as invested in the welfare of the other person as in self

- is neither angry nor dogmatic

- puts his or her energy into changing self rather than telling others what they should do

- is not influenced by the irresponsible opinions of others

- is clear about, and acts upon, his or her own values and principles, regardless of the behavior of the other person

In addition, this person is committed to a thoughtful response to any given situation, acting out of a desire to be authentic and live with integrity while remaining connected to the other. As a Christian, this person seeks above all to live out the calling God has on their lives, recognizing that God uses relationships to assist in this endeavor.

If you're thinking that these qualities describe Jesus, I agree! Jesus was the perfectly differentiated individual, and it is through His example and with the assistance of the Holy Spirit that we can actively seek to embody these characteristics in our own lives as well. This is the process of spiritual formation.

Detachment: A spiritual ideal

While the idea of differentiation is a powerful one, particularly in the way it is developed within the context of relationships, a related idea (and an ancient spiritual value) is that of detachment. Most of us hear the word "detached" and mistake it for disinterest or indifference. But that is a misunderstanding of the term. Taken within a spiritual context, detachment is the ability to act on clear principles and not be impelled by either your feelings or the opinions of others. This does not mean you don't listen to your feelings or are uninterested in the ideas of other people; it just means you don't allow them to cause you to act in ways that are not in keeping with your values.

An example of this can be seen in the case of "Sam," who discovers that his company is regularly defrauding its customers and decides to report this to the authorities. This would be a very difficult decision to make because the repercussions are frequently negative. He may wrestle with two conflicting values: his desire to provide for his family and his desire to behave in an ethical manner.

Furthermore, Sam's wife and family might urge him not to report the fraud because of the potential loss of his job or because his co-workers could make his life miserable. He would give up his dreams of being promoted in this company or of being hired by other companies, who might be wary of hiring a "whistle-blower." He would be viewed as a betrayer and a snitch by many people.

If the company goes out of business, others will lose their jobs. So in many ways, it would be easier to say nothing. And yet, by making this choice, he would be in collusion with the fraud. While he may not be perpetrating the act directly, by his silence he would be allowing it to continue. He would have to live with the knowledge that he allowed people to be victimized by his company while he did nothing to stop it.

This is exactly what a neighbor of ours faced when I was a child. He was a young and rising executive in a large company, with a wife and three children. He was also a committed Christian. I have no idea how long he wrestled with this decision, but he surely must have known the price he would pay for reporting the company. And indeed, the cost was tremendous. He lost his job, his home, and his profession. The family moved away. Later I learned that he was not able to find any job within his profession for several years; his career was destroyed.

This is a man who lived out his faith—who did not allow his feelings to dictate his actions. While I don't know what has become of him since then,

I do know that his case helped to bring about the current whistleblower laws that protect individuals who report such violations from the types of repercussions our neighbor faced. I trust that, despite the cost, he can sleep well at night knowing he took the narrow road. I believe that Christ was there with him through his darkest hours and that in the years since, he has reaped many blessings.

Balancing detachment and connection

This is a dramatic example of the idea of detachment, the goal of being unmoved by either the praise or criticism of others. Though you might think that detachment results in indifference to others, it in fact allows for an even deeper level of connection. Because you are not as invested in your own self-protection, in being right, or in defending yourself, you are better able to respond out of empathy and compassion.

As Alan Jones explains in his book *Soul Making,* there are two ways that are equally important in spiritual practice of detachment: "The first is the way of deep immersion and involvement in human experience; the second is that of radical separation from it."[1] This speaks to the ability to be fully present with another human being while at the same time being fully aware of one's own thoughts and feelings—a difficult goal but one that is worth striving for.

Differentiation and detachment: Two results of emotional and spiritual growth

Differentiation within the context of relationships is intimately related to the idea of detachment because if one is not moved by the praise or criticism of others, one will be able to remain in meaningful contact with difficult people and still be okay. Spiritual ideas can become vague and abstract if they are not placed within a context of human relationships. Thus I would argue that difficult relationships offer the best opportunity to develop the spiritual characteristic of detachment, along with the psychological goal of differentiation. And at this point, your relationship with your ex-spouse is most likely to be among the most challenging, so let's begin by examining the process by which you will change yourself in that relationship.

Shifting your perspective

The way we view an experience or a circumstance determines the way we respond to it. Imagine that you are driving on the freeway and another driver cuts you off. Most people will respond with anger at this apparently rude and inconsiderate behavior. But suppose you find out that the driver was rushing his pregnant wife to the hospital. Very likely, instead of feeling anger, you now feel compassion and empathy. Though the situation has not changed—the driver still cut you off—you no longer feel angry. What has changed is your perspective and that, in turn, has changed your response.

Shifting your perspective is the most powerful way to change your behavior because it is the most lasting. It is also the one thing you can always control. Most of us believe there is only one correct way to view a situation and only one right response. But in truth, there are any numbers of possibilities. Once you grasp this truth, you will begin to feel the empowerment it holds for you. No longer are you a victim of external circumstances (or an uncooperative ex-spouse!); you now hold the key to creating the life you want.

For example, let's say that you view your ex-spouse as controlling. From your perspective, he or she spends a lot of time and energy trying to get you and other people to do what they want—to follow some sort of script, like a director of a play guiding the actors on stage. When this happens, you likely feel angry and upset. "He is so controlling and manipulative!" "If she doesn't get her way, she makes everyone else miserable!" "I'm so tired of being pushed all the time!" And so it goes. Characterizing someone as controlling implies some kind of intentionality—that this person is selfish, inconsiderate, and thoughtless.

But what if instead of this person being controlling, you realized he or she is simply anxious? When Susan gets anxious, she tries to calm herself by getting everyone to follow her game plan. When John feels anxious, he pushes others to do what he wants. The behaviors are the same, but you may respond to them differently when seen from this perspective.

When people are afraid of loss, they get anxious. And when people become anxious, they engage in certain default behaviors to try to calm their anxiety. For some people, this translates into trying to control the world around them—including other people.

At this point, you may be thinking, *So what am I supposed to do? Just suck it up and do whatever he or she wants?* Not necessarily. This would be a no more thoughtful response than trying to get that person to stop trying to control others, an endeavor which in all likelihood you tried in your marriage. But this is how our minds seem to work—black and white, all or nothing responses. Either I stand up for myself and argue with him or her, or I stuff my feelings and go along to keep the peace. Both of these are reactions propelled by emotions rather than actions guided by thoughtful values.

An alternative to these two extremes requires that you stop expecting your ex-spouse to do anything differently than he or she has done in the past. It never ceases to amaze me how surprised married and formerly married couples can be at behaviors that have been consistent throughout their time together. If a person is consistently late for appointments, what causes us to think that he or she won't be late this time? Because we have gotten angry at them in the past for being late? Because we have pleaded with them to be on time? Because if they really loved us, they would stop being late?

The truth is that we spend an inordinate amount of time focusing on getting others to change—instructing, hinting, pleading, punishing—trying everything in our power to get that person to stop doing a behavior. This is what Bowen Family Systems calls an "anxious focus." We are anxiously focused on the other person, trying to get them to change instead of focusing on ourselves and determining what we will do differently. So in the above example, rather than trying to get the other person to be on time, we would decide what we will do *when* they are late. Not to try to get them to change (as in "I'll show him!"), but because we don't want to be late ourselves.

Now, however, you will want to decide how late is late. Being late for a strictly scheduled event like a flight to New York from Los Angeles is different than being late for a neighborhood open house. Ten or fifteen minutes might cost you a missed flight in the first instance, but carries a minimal or no cost in the second.

In order to change your part in the dance—that of the frustrated, angry individual waiting for the one-hundreth time for the other person to show up—you will need to prayerfully consider your values, some of which might be competing. And you will need to determine how flexible you can be, depending on the circumstances.

One of my clients had an ex-spouse who was highly unreliable, a characteristic that she had tried for fifteen years to change during their marriage—and continued to do so after their divorce. This caused her a great deal of frustration, anger, and righteous indignation. But her habitual responses—pleading, instructing, and threatening—had no more effect on him now than they did when they were married. This also caused an incredible amount of vitriol between the two of them, resulting in nasty fights and courtroom battles. Everyone lost.

Finally, my client became tired of the pointless battles that were only perpetuating her misery and were not creating the life she wanted, nor were they in keeping with the person she wanted to be. She and I worked to create a strategy for various repetitive situations; e.g., planning for him to be late or cancel at the last minute.

Our strategies focused on her behavior and what she would do to take care of herself and the children without being angry at her ex-spouse. For instance, when her ex-husband canceled plans at the last minute to pick up the children, my client decided that if she was going to be home anyway, she would accommodate the change by having the children stay at her house until he did come.

If she had plans to go out that evening, she would hire a babysitter and inform him that the sitter would be there when he came to pick up the kids. Given the predictability of his behavior, she had a list of sitters who could assist her at the last minute. She stopped yelling at him, griping about him to the kids, and in general stopped the vitriol and anger. Her life became much more peaceful as she became less focused on his behavior and gained more clarity on hers.

You may be thinking, *What about her ex-spouse? Why shouldn't he have to change?* Mainly because he didn't want to! He did not have a problem with his behavior—she did. All of her efforts to get him to change only resulted in her unhappiness.

Once she gave up that fruitless attempt, she felt empowered and free. She was no longer at the mercy of his decision not to change! She could decide to change herself. This effort was very challenging, and she did so with much prayer and support. She did not feel like accepting him as he is; she wanted him to be different. "It's not fair!" she'd say to me. "Why does he get things to go his way all the time?"

Her feelings impelled her toward anger so that she wouldn't be "walked on" by him. But the result was a lot of unnecessary anger, hurt, and recrimination with no change in his behavior. She alone held the key to her freedom and happiness.

Most people believe that circumstances are what determine their happiness. As a result, they spend a great deal of fruitless effort trying to change situations that can't be changed, change people who don't want to change, or change a past that is permanently fixed in time. My clients soon learn that while they can't always create the circumstances they want (though sometimes they can influence them), they can always determine their response to those circumstances.

For instance, you may not have wanted to get divorced and you may feel cheated out of the marriage you wanted to hold onto. You can continue to hold onto feelings of anger and resentment, to feel like a victim or a martyr. Or you can decide that you will cooperate with God in redeeming this experience of loss and grief. That is the choice you have and the empowerment that you alone can give yourself.

Changing your view of your ex-spouse

Choosing to see your divorce as a chance to grow is the starting point for the process of personal growth and spiritual formation. The next step is to change the way you think about your ex-spouse. Rather than viewing him or her as an enemy, imagine your ex-spouse as a tool to help you develop into the person you want to be. Like an exercise bike or a treadmill, your ex can give you an invaluable workout. Each encounter can take you in the direction of emotional growth and development.

At this point you may be thinking, *That might work for some people, but not in my case. You don't know my ex!* And you would be right—if your success depended on your ex-spouse. But you don't need the cooperation of anyone else to change your life, including your ex.

As you no doubt have learned by now, you cannot control the behavior of another person. When you try to do this, not only are you doomed to failure, you will also be perpetually frustrated. When you shift the focus onto your own behavior, you will discover true freedom and empowerment.

Try this experiment. Think of the last time you were angry with your former spouse. It may have been as recently as an hour ago. Replay the scene in your mind and observe the pattern of behavior between the two of you—this is the "dance" that you two return to again and again. Ask yourself, *What was my contribution to this dance? What was my intention in this conversation? What did I expect to happen?*

Observe the point at which you may have lost control and yelled or, conversely, gave up and shut down emotionally. Chances are that very little was resolved and both of you ended up feeling angry and frustrated. This is the result of what is called an "other-focused" interchange. During an other-focused conversation, your whole being is focused on the other person— what they are saying, how they are saying it, what they should be saying, etc.

Now replay this conversation again; instead of focusing on your former spouse, focus on yourself. What were you feeling? What did you want to accomplish? How did you want to feel? What you will notice is that your mind will quickly jump to the other. "I was feeling ticked off" (self-focus) "because he was being such a jerk!" (other focus). "I wanted a reasonable discussion" (self-focus), "but he was being controlling and manipulative as usual" (other focus). You can see how tied in you are—how dependent you are—on the other person in this scenario. True freedom, real independence, would be to have this same conversation, but instead of letting your feelings and thoughts be determined by your ex-spouse, they will be determined by you.

Easier said than done! But if you aim for this goal, the rewards will be inestimable. If you learn to be truly calm around this person (not the fake outward calm while you're boiling inside or when you're emotionally numb), you could be this way with any other person—your children, your parents, your next significant other.

As you learned in Chapter Nine, much of this will involve managing your biological response system—fight, flight, or freeze—as well as learning to identify and change your part in typical relationship patterns. This means you need to become aware of how your body feels when your limbic system is about to take over. You need to learn when you are about to hit the danger zone. And you need to recognize when your ex-spouse has crossed over that boundary as well.

When you think about the last argument you had with someone, recall the physical sensations you were experiencing. Rapid, shallow breathing and an increased heart rate are some of the signs that your limbic system is activated. Soon, thinking becomes difficult and you lose self-awareness; all your focus centers on the other person. In order to be successful in meeting the challenges of divorce, you will want to continue practicing techniques to help you manage your fight/flight/freeze mechanism. If you have done the exercises suggested at the end of Chapter Nine, you are on your way to learning to do this. Below are some further suggestions:

1. Make a list of your most deeply held values and principles. What kind of person do you want to be? What values do you have for yourself? How do you want to respond to others? What do you look like when you're at your best? Write a mission statement for yourself, starting with "I want to be a person who …."

2. Review your most recent intense emotional experiences in light of your list. At what point did you behave in ways not in keeping

with your values? What did the other person say or do to push your emotional buttons? When did you change from feeling calm to upset? What was the trigger point?

3. Plan for the next time. Based on the information you have gathered, what will you do to behave in ways that are consistent with your principles or values? Some ideas include:

a. Stop the conversation earlier. Say something like, "I'm feeling overwhelmed; I need to stop now" can be helpful. Avoid saying something about the other person, such as, "You're out of control." This will only escalate the emotional intensity.

b. Take some deep breaths and focus on your breathing. Periodically check in with yourself during the conversation. Taking a few deep, slow breaths will help you calm yourself and enable you to think more clearly.

c. Practice the breath prayer. As you are breathing, think about your breath prayer—the traditional Jesus prayer may be the one you selected: "Lord Jesus Christ, Son of God, have mercy on me." Repeat this until you feel calm. The breath prayer not only helps you refocus your attention, it also opens you up to the work of the Holy Spirit.

d. Plan ahead and strategize. By now, you know how many of your conversations are likely to play out. So have a game plan for what you will say and do. If, for instance, you want to talk about child visitation arrangements, plan for your ex-spouse's possible responses and how you might respond in turn.

e. Take a clear position about yourself. If your position is that you don't want to get into an argument, what will you do to make that happen? What is your ex likely to do get you off your position? Let's say you're having a discussion and you realize that you are having difficulty remaining calm. Your best response might be to take a break and try again later. Your ex may say something like, "You always do this. You just want to control everything." Your response might be, "That's the way it seems to you, but I'm still going to take a break. This isn't working for me right now; when can we talk again?" You might have to repeat this a few times. If the other person is insistent, you may decide to say something like, "Okay. I'll call you tomorrow and see if we can set up a time." And then hang up or leave. Staying will only result in having the argument you don't want to have.

f. Whenever possible, think of a reframe. Reframing is a useful way to change your perspective on any situation. Individuals tend to negatively stereotype their ex-spouses: "He's such a jerk"; "She's such a control freak"; "He's so inconsiderate"; "She's crazy." When you have these thoughts, there's really no way to have a reasonable conversation with the other person. Your attitude will come through loud and clear. Knowing what you now know about the brain and how it works, you can see that we all are largely guided by our limbic system, which means that much of the time we're not really thinking, we're reacting. This is true of your ex as well. So thinking of this person as reactive or anxious, rather than as a jerk or control freak, can help you become less reactive yourself.

4. Practice these techniques with others. Your ex-spouse is not the only person who challenges you. Your children, your parents, your siblings—in fact, any relationship that is important to you—will offer you an opportunity to grow yourself.

The key to success in this undertaking is to take it one step at a time, one skill at a time. Otherwise, it is too easy to become discouraged and give up. Sometimes a client will come back to me and say, "I did what you said and it didn't work." And I'll ask how they know this. Inevitably the client will respond, "Because my ex-spouse was just as nasty as ever." In other words, the other person didn't change. This is when I know that we need to revisit the goal, which is to change yourself, not the other person.

Success lies in making small, incremental changes. So if you, like my client, become discouraged because you tried a new skill and your spouse did not change his or her typical response, ask yourself, *Did I remain calm and thoughtful? Instead of jumping into an argument, did I calmly disengage? Did I identify a position and attempt to keep the focus on that?* If so, then count that as a success. Just as you wouldn't expect to run a marathon after one day of jogging, don't expect that you will see your efforts bear fruit with your first attempt to change yourself with your ex-spouse. But if you continue to follow the guidelines outlined above, over time you will see a lowering of intensity in all your relationships.

What does this process look like?

If you're like me, it's sometimes hard to incorporate new ideas into your life when you don't have a clear picture of the outcome. It's all well and good to talk about responding calmly to an angry ex-spouse and avoid getting into arguments, but putting that into practice is not that easy. In addition, you don't want to necessarily go along with everything your ex-spouse demands of you. Remember: The goal is to be authentic, fully who you are while you're in connection with your ex-spouse. So defaulting to just giving in would mean you're not being authentic.

In fact, by just giving into his or her demands, in effect you're lying to keep the peace—and dishonesty is contrary to Christian values. So how do you hold on to who you are while in connection with your ex? Below are a few examples that may assist your understanding of this concept.

Susan — Learning to become more present in her relationships

Susan came to see me after her husband of twenty years left her for another woman. Susan's marriage had been characterized by times of intense conflict followed by periods of relative calm, and there was an emotional disconnect between Susan and her husband Nick. Susan had been a stay-at-home mom, pouring herself into the activities of her two children, a son now twenty and a sixteen-year-old daughter. Her husband was a busy executive in a major corporation and he traveled a lot on business. Over the years, Susan had become increasingly dissatisfied with her husband's lack of involvement in family activities, and she felt burdened with the responsibilities of parenting their children. Her pattern had been to stuff her feelings and thoughts inside until finally she would explode.

At first, Susan and Nick had come in to see me together, but it soon became apparent that Nick was not really interested in changing himself. He believed he had found the answer to his problems with this new relationship, and I got the impression that he was handing his wife over to me so he could move on. Though Susan was desperate to save her marriage, it quickly became clear to both of us that what she really wanted was a new marriage—hopefully with Nick.

Our work together really began once Susan started to identify the typical patterns of interaction in her marriage. For the first week, I suggested that she just observe herself in her relationship with Nick. What Susan discovered was a strong tendency to deny her own desires, even to herself; this created a pattern in which she would ignore her own feelings or thoughts and then blow up at him for being selfish and inconsiderate.

Another pattern that Susan identified was her consistent efforts to try to manage the emotional reactions of others, particularly those of her husband, in order to avoid an upset. "I feel like I'm walking around on eggshells a lot of the time," she explained.

The next step was to assist Susan in identifying some of her values and principles. She knew, for instance, that she did not want to be the type of wife or mother who consistently blew up at her husband or kids. Nor did she want to continue to be oblivious to her own needs and desires. Instead, she wanted to be a woman who had the self-confidence to be clear about what she wanted without trampling on the rights of others. In addition, she wanted to learn to have conflict without wounding those she loved.

The more Susan focused on what she wanted to change about herself, the less intense her relationships became. She began by working on her responses to her husband. Rather than just defaulting to whatever Nick wanted, or, conversely, blowing up at him, she started to become curious about him and his thinking. She realized that she was often confused by his behavior and reacted to that by becoming frustrated. Now, she was more likely to ask him a question and explore his thinking.

She also began to state more clearly what she was or was not willing to live with; in other words, she began to learn to take a position. For example, she told Nick that since they were no longer living as husband and wife, she would prefer that he stop dropping by the house without calling first. She was able to state this request factually, knowing that she was prepared to change the locks on the house if he decided not to honor her request. If she did that, she would need to follow through without anger or acrimony. Otherwise, it would come across as a threat rather than a position.

As her relationship with Nick became less contentious, Susan was able to see her marriage to him more clearly. While there had been a number of strengths in their relationship, she had felt lonely much of the time. Moreover, she began to observe how condescending Nick had been to her and that she often felt as though she were his inferior. Consequently she developed some empathy for Nick, seeing his condescension as a cover-up for his own insecurities.

At the same time, she became aware of a part of her that agreed with him. In other words, she, too, had a tendency to see herself as intellectually inferior to others and thus Nick's assessment of her had hit home. Understanding this gave Susan an ability to see him in a different light. Rather than seeing Nick as a cold, condescending man, she was able to view him as an individual who could not tolerate true emotional closeness. She knew she wanted more from a marriage than what she had once had with Nick, but she also knew that she would need to continue to grow herself in order to make that happen.

Eventually Nick filed for divorce and this was a very difficult time for Susan. Some part of her had hoped that he might change his mind and recommit to the marriage. Over time, she processed her grief and slowly began to accept the fact that their marriage was over. She began to reconnect with her siblings with whom she had a distant relationship, and she maintained positive connections with her in-laws. She avoided bad-mouthing her ex-husband, knowing that this would only injure her children as they struggled to come to terms with the divorce.

Over time, she came to see Nick as someone who would always be part of her family as her co-parent and the two of them were able to establish a cordial, workable relationship. That this occurred was due in large part to Susan's hard work and efforts. She bore the brunt of the pain and grief in the divorce and it would have been easy to descend into angry retribution in response to her hurt.

Her husband acted dishonorably with little regard for her or the children when he left the family and moved in with his girlfriend. It was tempting to "make him pay" for the hurt he had caused her. Yet Susan knew, too, that such a response would only cause more damage in the long run for all concerned. Though she had not been a church-going person, early in the process, she began to read a prayer book that her mother had left her and found these to be soothing and comforting. I know that God used her willingness to put aside her own hurt and pain to the benefit of her children. And because she was willing to place her husband's well-being on a par with her own, she is now enjoying the rewards of that decision. Life is better for Susan than it once was, even though it is not the life she would have planned for herself twenty years ago.

One advantage that Susan did have was an ex-spouse who was not vindictive or abusive. Despite the fact that he effectively abandoned Susan and her family, he maintained regular contact with her and the children and did not begrudge her spousal and child support. In this way, he was extremely generous. Many spouses who leave their families add insult to injury by fighting for custody, hiding financial resources, deliberately quitting their jobs in order to be unemployed and thus unable to pay support—the list goes on. Research has shown that this phenomenon is all too common. So while you might think that the person who leaves his or her spouse for another person would feel guilty and act out of kindness to try to make up for the injury, just the opposite is more often the case.

But whether or not you or your spouse initiated the divorce, you may find yourself trying to co-parent with an uncooperative ex-spouse. I have worked with many clients in this situation. In each case, we were able to settle down the intensity in that relationship and make life, if not peaceful, at least less chaotic and contentious.

Jennifer – Learning to manage custody challenges

Even in the best of divorces, custody arrangements can raise anxiety and create ongoing difficulties. Usually these occur when one of you wants to change a previously agreed upon schedule. For instance, your ex-spouse wants to have the children stay with them for a couple of extra days, or you want to take the kids on a trip during the time your spouse would normally have them. These requests stir up a lot of hot emotions: old hurts from the divorce, fears that the children prefer your spouse, anxiety about whether or not your spouse will try to sue for full custody, anger over paying child support, feeling taken advantage of—this list goes on.

Ironically, this issue is the cause for most of the damage done to children in a divorce, as custody battles can be the most wounding of all divorce-related issues. I've heard of family court judges who are so tired of couples fighting over the kids that they order ridiculous custody arrangements—half the week with one spouse and half with the other. So the children end up shuttling back and forth between two different households every few days—a situation made all the more difficult when the two parents continue to battle outside the courtroom.

As a Christian, it is of utmost importance that you resolve not to put your children through this experience, regardless of the behavior of your spouse. Do not let his or her threats, or anger, or poor behavior allow you to descend into similar responses. In fact, the less threatening you are to your ex-spouse, the less likely you are to be threatened in return. This is one truth where you will have to trust God and take an active step forward in faith because everything in our culture—and our human nature—says to fight back.

In the vast majority of cases, however, custody arrangements are already codified in family law and judges are highly reluctant to change these unless there are very good reasons to do so—things like outright physical abuse and neglect on the part of one of the parents. In these cases, a psychologist will do an evaluation of each of the parents and the children and recommend the best custody arrangement to the court.

Most of the time, however, differences in ideas about parenting account for custody battles. One client of mine, Jennifer, was ready to go to court because her ex-husband insisted that her son play soccer when her son did not want to. While I understand the desire to protect her children from emotional pain and frustration, this situation does not qualify as child abuse.

Jennifer's marriage had been difficult from the start and only got worse over the years. Eventually Jennifer's husband decided to file for divorce. Despite my suggestion to use a mediator, Jennifer felt so threatened and angry that she ran to the nearest divorce attorney who quickly amped up Jennifer's anxiety. He urged her to document everything her husband said or did, to stay in the house despite the fact that the two of them had become so intense with each other that Jennifer locked herself in her bedroom several times, and to hire an expensive forensic accountant.

Meanwhile, her husband retaliated by accusing Jennifer of being an alcoholic and an unfit mother. She and the children had to go through a court-ordered evaluation. One year and $100,000 in attorneys' fees later, Jennifer ended up with essentially the same arrangement as she would have if she had used a mediator.

My client's upset over this situation actually made things worse for her son. In time, she was able to let go of her anxiety over this situation and strategize some alternative responses with her son, one of which is to learn how to make the best of a situation—a life lesson.

The two of them sat down and looked at what he did like about soccer: He had some friends on the team, he liked being outside, and it was one of the few times his dad actively participated in his life. Once my client settled herself down, her son was able to have a fairly enjoyable time in soccer that season, and by the time the next season rolled around, soccer was no longer so important to her ex-husband and the issue did not come up again.

What Jennifer came to understand is that her upset with her ex-husband was fueling her son's anxiety. He felt that he had to side with his mother and protect her from his father. As the oldest of three children, Jennifer's son was in danger of being placed in the role of pseudo-husband, and I pointed this out to her. She recalled playing a similar role with her parents, trying to mediate their fights and feeling responsible for her alcoholic mother.

My client's decision to settle herself down and lower the intensity in the relationship with her ex-husband is an example of what is called a "differentiating move." She responded differently than her family system pulled her to respond. In so doing, she was able to reassure her son that she could take care of herself and did not need him to be responsible for her. And she was able to back her words up with behaviors.

She did this by taking the focus off her ex-husband, which in the past had resulted in her constant worrying about what he would do next and her continued attempts to get him to change. Instead she was able to formulate a calm, thoughtful response. She and I indentified some of the typical behaviors of her ex-husband and what she might do to change her habitual pattern of reacting.

One thing she identified was his tendency to change plans at the last minute. This had been a constant challenge for her in their marriage, and yet she continued to act surprised when it happened. She would become angry and frustrated, telling herself, *How could he be so thoughtless!* and *He's got to understand what he's doing to me and the kids!*

She vacillated between anger and the belief that she could somehow get him to change. Giving up this belief was very difficult for Jennifer because it was one she had carried with her from her childhood. It made her feel safe and in control, despite the fact that the opposite was in fact the case; believing she could change someone only made her feel vulnerable and out of control. Once she gave up this belief, she and I strategized some alternative responses to his being late and changing plans. She began by predicting how he might act in any situation.

For instance, if it was his night to pick up the kids for soccer practice, she predicted that he was (a) highly likely to be late, or (b) call at the last minute and say he couldn't make it, and/or (c) forget to bring their equipment. She then came up with plans A, B and C. If he was late, she would expect him to explain to the coach. If the coach called her instead (which had been the case in the past), she would give him her ex-husband's phone number and suggest he talk to him. If he called and said he couldn't make it, she would take the kids herself if she was available. If not, she created a back-up plan to have her kids carpool with another parent. She also decided that the kids would have a set of their soccer gear at her house and that the children were responsible for remembering to take it to practices and games.

At first, her ex-husband became angry when she refused to call the coach. But rather than engage him in an argument to "try to get him to understand that he needed to take responsibility," she simply restated her position calmly. If he started yelling, she told him she was going to hang up the phone at that point since the current conversation not going to get them anywhere.

He texted and emailed angry messages to her, threatening to go back to court for another custody battle, calling her an uncaring mother, and using everything he knew to try to get her to engage in another fight. Instead, she either ignored the message or responded only to the factual part of the message: "You want to pick up the kids at 10 a.m. on Saturday. I will have them ready for you at that time"—all without any further words or explanation.

Over time, things settled down significantly, though it took at least a month or more of her sticking to her position. She, in turn, became calmer and less anxious as a result of her efforts. During this time, she focused on her spiritual practice of daily prayer and also began using the breath prayer, which helped her calm herself and refocus her thoughts during the most difficult interchanges with her husband.

Slowly, she began to see that her goal of trying to get her ex-husband to realize how awful he was behaving was working. He eventually realized he needed to be more mature, arrive on time, and stop canceling at the last minute. All the behaviors she had wanted him to change during their fifteen years of marriage were finally changing. Her earlier efforts had not only been futile, they had also destroyed her ability to create a fulfilling and rewarding life for herself.

Consequently, she began to seek her own path and listen to the still, small voice of God for direction. Jennifer was able to see how her willingness to take a step of faith, to trust God in the process, and to practice her beliefs in tangible ways resulted in a deeper, more rewarding relationship with her children, family, and friends.

Donna — Learning to take a position while being flexible

Another issue that is a frequent source of contention involves time with the children. Men are often concerned that their ex-wives are going to sue for full custody, and in the past this was often granted since the assumption was that children needed their mother more than their father. Now, however, most couples have something closer to a 50/50 custody arrangement, though it is still common for the children to spend more time with the mother in order to maintain consistency in school attendance. But whatever the formal arrangement is, life has a way of intruding on the best laid plans.

Since most divorces involve the use of attorneys, by the time the divorce occurs it is highly likely that the former spouses now see each other as the enemy. If this describes your situation, you will need to be willing to give up that perspective for the sake of your children—and for your own spiritual development. If you see your ex-spouse as a threat, then it will be very difficult, if not impossible, to work with him or her on co-parenting your children. In addition, any requests that your ex will make are likely to be interpreted with suspicion and distrust. This, too, will create challenges in responding with a calm, non-anxious attitude.

Understanding that your children need and love both parents and putting that thought ahead of your own wants and desires is the most difficult aspect of parenthood—even in the best of situations. It is all the more important when parents are divorced. But it is imperative that at least one parent—in this case, you—act on that, which means there will be many times when your children will want to see your ex when you had other plans. This is not to say that you allow your children to make these decisions but that you seek their input when making your decisions. Again, a prayerful response—one that is truly rooted in a value or principle—is one that takes into account the well-being of all concerned.

My client, Donna, has done an excellent job of balancing out the needs of her children to be with their father with their need to be with her and to maintain commitments to school and other activities. Donna and her ex-husband divorced using a mediator rather than attorneys. As a result, they have complete freedom to determine how they will handle the custody of their children. Using a mediator prevented the divorce from escalating into a battleground and allowed them to emerge from the process as cordial co-parents.

Donna's ex-husband has a demanding, unstructured work schedule, so there have been times when he has an unexpected week off and he has asked to have the children at his house during that time. Initially, Donna was upset by his requests, though this had been an old, familiar pattern. She believed that he frequently got his own way and she ended up on the short end of the stick.

But as she and I processed this assumption and she worked to clarify her values as a Christian, she was able to let go of this belief, instead letting each request be considered on its own merits. So there were times when she said "no" because her older son had made plans that week, or they had just been at their dad's house, or she needed to be out of town the following week. But there were other times she said "yes" when her sons wanted to be with their dad that week and nothing important was on the schedule.

There were other instances when one son wanted to go and the other didn't, or they would spend part of the week with their dad and part of it at her house. The possibilities were endless. They have both maintained a regular custody schedule, so these requests were outside of the agreed upon arrangement.

Donna's commitment to redeeming her divorce experience by allowing God to use it for her highest good has resulted in a life that is more fulfilling than she had ever imagined. In addition, her children have not had to endure the wounds that come from being caught up in custody battles and being used as pawns as each parent tries to "win" the divorce. The narrow road may seem difficult or even impossible at first, but the rewards for having the courage to take it are everlasting.

Walking the talk: Taking the narrow road through the journey of divorce

There is no way to do justice to the hard work, courage, and determination of the clients whose stories you have just read. Each of these cases represents at least a year of consistent effort in changing long-standing habits and reactions. But as I tell my clients: Even the smallest of changes on your part will have big results in the long run. You are not required to try to become someone you are not. God will use your efforts to help you become more fully who you are!

But the journey of spiritual formation is indeed just that—a journey. It is a process by which, day by day, you become transformed. You will become a person who will more naturally respond as Christ would to a circumstance or, in this case, to a challenging ex-spouse.

In addition, you will be changing your children's emotional inheritance. By lowering the intensity of your reactions to your ex-spouse, as well as to others in your family, you will be creating a different family system than the one in which you grew up. Your children and grandchildren, and all who will follow, will enjoy the benefits of your hard work and determination. To paraphrase Proverbs 31:28: "They will rise up and call you blessed."

1. Implementing what you have learned in this chapter, set aside time each day this week to work on some of the most repetitive issues you have with your ex-spouse. Start by making a list. Next, review your list and circle two or three of the most challenging. Explore each of these by writing about the "dance" the two of you tend to repeat. Underline your part in the dance. Next, prayerfully

consider some alternative responses, keeping in mind the idea of a calm, non-anxious response that is based on a principle or value—not on trying to get your ex-spouse to change. Make a list of these responses and commit to implementing them in the next month. If you do not have a professional counselor, be open to finding someone who can coach you through your strategies.

2. Like many of us, you may find that setting aside regular time each day for prayer and contemplation is a challenge. And yet you cannot do the work that is required of you without the underpinning of prayer and meditation. Take a few moments to identify these challenges in your own life. Is it finding the time? Is it an unwillingness to surrender and trust? Is it a fear of what you might discover about yourself? Or of painful feelings and memories that might arise? Read Psalm 139:1–18. What comes to mind as you think about God's knowing you? How might you bring this concern before God in your prayer today?

CHAPTER TWELVE

Finding Goodness
(Melissa's Story)

I am still confident of this:
I will see the goodness of the LORD
in the land of the living.
—Psalm 27:13–14

Looking back at how far I've come, it's just amazing to me how God can use so much pain and suffering to create so much good. It has been quite a journey for me, and for a time I was in the deepest, darkest depths. I was Jonah in the belly of the whale—terrified, feeling so alone, finally emerging from the utter darkness, bruised and battered but willing to take those first shaky steps in the right direction.

My journey began about 11 years ago when I first discovered my husband was having an affair. We had been married for about sixteen years at that time and had three daughters. The oldest, whom I had prior to my marriage to my husband, was already an adult at that time.

I confronted my husband once I found out about the affair with his secretary, and he just told me, "Okay, I'm not going to see her anymore. It's all over." In hindsight, I should have insisted that some obvious changes be made, but instead, I just willingly accepted what he told me.

So there was really no time of healing, of really working out what brought the affair into our marriage, or of us working things out as a couple. We did go to counseling for a few sessions, but he didn't want to go back and, truthfully, I think I was afraid what I might discover, so I readily agreed not to return to counseling. I was afraid of where that might take us.

But I knew somewhere in the regions of my heart that the affair continued. We would go to functions at his company and other people would say things like, "She's the most important person to him," hinting without coming right out and saying it. Emotionally, though, it was taking its toll on me. It got to the point where I would ask him every two months if he was still having the affair. His answer was always, "No! It's all in your mind. You're making it up. It's not true," which was really abusive, since he was lying.

Then my husband and I attended a company party during which she sang a song for him. I finally realized something was up. I thought, *I'm losing my mind. Either I'm crazy or there is something here that I don't understand.* And so, on the recommendation of my boss, I went away to a treatment clinic for about a week and a half. I had twice daily sessions with the psychologist who ran the clinic and then group sessions throughout the day, as well as a one-on-one session with someone who had been through the program. It was wonderful for me. It helped me to come to grips with a lot of feelings, lots of old history. When I returned home, I had a previously scheduled operation for a tumor in my uterus. I ended up having some complications from the surgery and was totally unable to function for about a month and a half. I think the emotional strain I had been living under was taking its toll on me physically.

Still, I really held out hope for my marriage. I was still convalescing during the holidays, but I had a friend pick me up and drive me to the place where my husband purchased his suits and shirts. Even though I could walk only a few steps, I went in and sat down and ordered two suits and matching shirts and ties for Christmas. I thought that if I bought him enough— made him happy—he'd choose me and stay.

But he didn't buy me a gift. He spent a lot of time away. And it was at Christmas that we finally had this huge confrontation. "I don't love you anymore," he announced. "I care about what happens to you, but I don't love you. I'm in love with Denise." And I just fell apart. Everything I had was being taken away from me. I worked for a church at the time, and my boss suggested that perhaps I should find another job. So now I had no job and my marriage was dissolving, so I just went into survival mode.

I started looking for another job. My husband decided to sleep in another bedroom and think about what he wanted, what would make him happy. Our two kids knew something was going on! It was a really confusing time, and I was still recovering from my surgery. I was still not able to drive, so if I went to work, my husband would have to take me.

I had very few support resources in place at that time, which made it all the more difficult. At the end of my time at the treatment facility, the psychologist had urged me to find a 12-step group as soon as possible, as well as start working with a therapist. But because of the surgery, I wasn't able to do that.

However, after I found a new job, I got on the phone and started looking for a 12-step group. I was looking for one that dealt with codependency issues but one that wasn't going to just be a gripe session. I wanted to be with people who were sharing their recovery and talked about how they made the steps and were moving forward. So I found a 12-step writing workshop at a local hospital. There were about forty people and we were divided into ten groups.

I know that God was a part of that because I remember sitting there and selecting those people whom I did not want to be in a group with. As we sat around and shared, I thought, *Mmmm, I don't want to be with her. I don't want to be with him.* And every single person I had pointed to ended up in my group. That group had all the dynamics that I needed to face, and they became a family to me.

I started going there every week, and I also found a separate CoDA (Co-Dependents Anonymous) sharing group. In addition, I searched for a therapist, and I went to him a couple of times. (I even got my husband to attend once.) But I was still very fragile, and I was not ready to hear the things the counselor said, like, "He's been having this affair for two years. You don't matter to him," etc. So I fell apart.

It was at this time that I suffered one more incredible loss. My best friend died of breast cancer. That was on a Wednesday night, and my husband moved out the next morning. I had come home late that night and found him still up, waiting for me to arrive. The next morning, the grief of my friend's death really hit me, and I started to cry. I took a shower to try to stop the tears. When I got out of the shower, I heard the garage door shutting. He was leaving. I found out later that Denise, his girlfriend, had been with him that evening in the downstairs bedroom!

So he packed up that day and moved out. I found another counselor, and that was the person I ultimately stayed with. She agreed to see my husband and me and, though he said he would not have contact with Denise and that he would try to work on our marriage, it only took her two sessions to figure out that he was still seeing her. So we just started working on me.

Still, that was the beginning of my deepest despair; it was my dark night of the soul. Somehow, I managed to get through my best friend's funeral service, but a week later, I took all the steps to take my life. I lined up all the pills, the glasses of water, and had it ready to go. I put my kids to bed, but I began to think of how they would find me, and I knew I couldn't do that to them. So I called my sister, who lives about an hour or so away, and I said, "I have everything here and this is what I'm going to do, but I don't know what to do about the kids. I want somebody here."

I thought I would have somebody here to be with my kids! She made me promise not to take my life but to wait two hours and then call her again. During those two hours, she called my older daughter, who got in her car and came over. She sat with me, talked to me, got me to call my therapist, to call my friends from my 12-step group, and talk to them. They, along with my therapist, got me through that time. I made an agreement with my therapist that if I ever got to that place again, I would call her and let her know.

I decided, at that moment, that I would survive. I thought to myself, *Okay. Somehow, this is going to work.* It was my conscious choice that that had to happen. I knew I had to do something, and I did. I continued to attend my therapy sessions and went to my CoDA support group. They really became my family in some ways. They were a family system that I could function in. I could say what I felt or what I thought; in my original family system that was not allowed. The support group helped me put into practice what I was learning with my therapist.

I also decided I needed to get some kind of work, even though some people advised me not to in order to get more spousal and child support. But I knew I needed to get out and be with people. I found a part-time clerical position with a church. They knew my skills and my experience, but they didn't know that I was struggling in my marriage.

I needed a place to take a break from all that, so I decided not to tell them at first. I started working on January 24th and he moved out on February 18th. So I had been working there for about a month when it hit—the real yuck hit. I would come to work and sit down at my desk, and then I would get up and go to the bathroom and cry. Then I'd clean my face, and go back to my desk and work for another half hour or so before I went back to the bathroom to cry some more.

Eventually, someone got wind that something was really wrong and they told our pastor, who called me into his office. "What's going on?" he asked. I told him and he was so supportive. He told me to read the Psalms, because no one would help me through my pain and hurt like David. And he told me to read *Love Must Be Tough* by James Dobson, which I read that night. It was the first time somebody put into words what I needed to do when I first found out about my husband's affair.

In reading the Psalms, God gave me the words from Psalm 27:13 and 14: "I am still confident of this: I will see the goodness of the LORD in the land of the living. Wait for the LORD; be strong and take heart and wait for the LORD." That has been my life verse since my divorce. God has promised me the goodness of the Lord, not just in heaven, but in the land of the living.

My job was one area where I really received some positive recognition for who I am and for my talents and abilities. I moved up from a part-time clerical position to where I am now, overseeing an important part of a very large ministry. Before my divorce, I had always defined myself by the man I was with. Being a married woman, being someone's wife, had very high value to me. I was a very young, older woman. I think that a big part of what has brought me to the place I am now—where I really have value just for who I am with no other attachments—is learning that I could do things on my own. Now I am very comfortable being me. I find I have worthiness and value on my own.

My daughters will tell you that our relationship has changed, too. I value them. I love them. I want to be with them, but they are not my representation of me in the world. I am much less critical, less judgmental of them. I am much more likely to look for the cause rather than for who is to blame. And my kids are doing great.

One daughter is graduating from Northwestern University and my youngest is now in eighth grade and an honor student. I have some wonderful friends. I never had a brother, but out of that CoDA workshop, I acquired a brother who is just my rock. I can talk to him about anything. I've got two strong friends in my life who I can call whenever I need to.

In fact, when I recently broke off an engagement, I got on the phone and called one of my friends. "I need you now," I said. And she came. She sat on the floor and held me and cried with me. God has given me great gifts. So I've learned the extreme value of relationships through all this. I have a gathering of relationships that are important, that feed my soul. I've learned that this is how God works. We are God's arms. We are the physical touch. He made us to need it.

And now I am open to allowing Him to use me in any way He can. I believe my greatest joy over the past ten years is that I have realized the potential within me—what I could do, who I was. I am doing what I love. It enriches me and lifts me. And I would never have found it if I hadn't gone through my divorce. Just like Joseph, who had to go through so much in order to be where God wanted him to be, how else could I have been here unless I had gone through what I did? For this time in my life, I am Joseph, who used his talents to serve God and His people.

REFLECTION

Of all the stories presented herein, Melissa's presents the descent to the depths in the most dramatic fashion: her attempted suicide. No other impulse signifies the need for a dramatic change in one's life more vividly. As James Hillman explains in his book *Suicide and the Soul*, "Any careful consideration of life entails reflections of death, and the confrontation with reality means facing mortality. We never come fully to grips with life until we are willing to wrestle with death."[1]

Later he elaborates: "The impulse to death need not be conceived as an anti-life movement; it may be a demand for an encounter with absolute reality, a demand for a fuller life through the death experience."[2] Thus, suicide can be said to be a dramatic siren warning of the imminent need for a death (the end of the old life) so a new life can emerge. The mistake we make is to literalize this impulse when often what is needed is a significant change in our way of being in the world.

This is what Melissa's suicide attempt accomplished for her. From the moment she said to herself, *Okay, somehow, this is going to work,* Melissa embarked upon a course that would take her to a new experience of life. No longer a "young" girl in a woman's body who defines herself only by the man in her life, Melissa has forged a life that includes the expression of latent talents and abilities as well as the knowledge that she can provide all that she needs for herself. Now she is more aware of her true self, with all the flaws and the wounds, as well as the strengths and the beauty. Out of the very depths of life, having looked death in the face, Melissa emerges as a person transformed—one who can now give to others out of the lessons gleaned from her experience.

For Melissa, as for most of the women in this study, the figure of Joseph is a recurring archetype. Joseph can be seen as a heroic figure who endures much suffering, after which he rises out of the depths to a new life, one in which the ultimate meaning and purpose of his existence is revealed. For these women, the story of Joseph gave both hope for a new life as well as an example of grace and forgiveness.

But another figure also offers an interesting illumination of these stories and that is the ancient Greek character of Psyche. She, too, is heroic, but
in a way that is essentially feminine, and thus fundamentally different from
the masculine approach. In Jungian psychology, masculine and feminine
speak of inner characteristics that are common to both males and females.

The masculine aspect can be described as focused attention, goal-ori-
ented, and linear in approach, whereas the feminine aspect is characterized
by receptivity, patience, compassion, nourishing, relatedness to others. In
our culture, the masculine characteristics are generally encouraged if one is
to meet societal standards of success. As a consequence, many people in our
culture—both men and women—denigrate much of what is characteristic
of the feminine. Receptivity is miscast as passivity; nourishing is dismissed
in favor of external accomplishment. But both feminine and masculine attitudes are necessary for a person to live life in a way that is both fulfilling
and meaningful. And this is what Psyche's story points to: In the interplay
between the masculine and the feminine something new can be created.

In this story, Aphrodite gives Psyche four impossibly challenging tasks to
complete that speak to the challenges of grief in divorce. The first task is that
of sorting an overwhelming number of seeds. Both Psyche and Aphrodite are
sure this is an impossible challenge. At first, Psyche despairs. But just at the
moment when she is at a loss, an ant appears and persuades its compatriots to
take pity on the girl, and together they work to sort the seeds into piles.

When viewed in light of the grief of divorce, this first task can be
understood as the initial confusion and despair individuals face when confronted with the decision to leave a marriage or when their spouse tells them
they want a divorce.

It is significant that what assists Psyche is a creature from the world of
nature. Such a figure represents the instinctual nature that each of us must
have access to if we are to become whole—the intuitive wisdom that comes
from beyond our intellect, given to us by God. The first stage of grief, and
of transformation, is characterized by darkness and confusion. What this
tells us is that what will help us bring some order and light into the darkness

The Grace-Filled Divorce   185

is to avail ourselves of our instinctual nature, which often resides in the shadows of our psyche.

The second task that Psyche faces involves going to a field and gathering some golden fleece from rams that pasture there. As she approaches the field, she encounters some reeds in a river who warn her of the destructive power of these sheep and she, once again, despairs. But the reeds advise her to wait until nightfall during which time the rams are no longer there, and she can then gather some of the fleece off the brambles and boughs.

Again, the voice of nature—this time tied to water, which is a symbol of the unconscious—assists Psyche in completing her task. The ram is representative of masculine power that can be destructive if not handled carefully. To approach it directly is foolhardy, but when one is respectful of this characteristic of the masculine and comes at it in a subtle manner, then it can be of great service.

As Robert Johnson notes, "Our myth cautions us to take the power we need, sacrifice what is not required and keep power and relatedness in proportion."[3] This means that we must use the masculine energy as a tool and not allow it to take over and destroy our capacity for relatedness. If we do not balance these forces, then we are likely to face a destructive and wounding divorce.

The third task involves another dangerous undertaking. Aphrodite, by now enraged at Psyche's successes, has ordered her to fill a crystal goblet with water from the Styx, the river that flows down to the gates of hell. But the river is guarded by dangerous monsters and it is impossible to set foot close enough to dip the goblet into the water. This time, an eagle sent by Zeus assists Psyche by taking the goblet from her and dipping it into the stream. He brings the goblet back to Psyche and her task is completed.

In each task, Psyche is a little more conscious and in this one, it is the spiritual principle that assists her. Now Psyche can receive the masculine impulse and give it form without being destroyed by it. One must have the higher perspective, the ability to see beyond the immediate circumstances, like an eagle, who can take in a much larger landscape than we who are earthbound can.

From this vantage, we can see the next step to take and then begin by taking that step, not trying to do the journey all at once.

Melissa relates how she was advised not to go to work in order to increase the spousal support she might receive, but she followed her instinct instead and found a part-time position, knowing that it was a matter of life and death to do so. Not only did this first step assist in her initial healing, it later became the entrée toward a career that has been fulfilling because of her talents and abilities. This is a woman following both an instinct and a higher calling. It is the eagle energy that shows us the next step to take as well as the possibilities for the future.

The fourth and final task is the most important and difficult of all. Psyche is instructed to go into the underworld and ask Persephone, the goddess who resides there, for a cask of her beauty ointment, which Psyche is then to deliver to Aphrodite.

In great despair when faced with the impossibility of this task, Psyche flees to a tower in order to throw herself off. But it is at this point that she receives the instructions from the tower that will help her navigate this task. These instructions are detailed and elaborate, but Psyche is able to follow them and returns with the cask. But though the tower has instructed her not to open the cask, Psyche, overwhelmed with desire to use the contents of the cask to woo her beloved Eros, disobeys. She opens the box and discovers that there is nothing there. What emanates, however, is a deadly sleep, which overcomes Psyche. She is rescued by Eros, who admonishes her for her curiosity and instructs her to proceed with the cask and give it to Aphrodite. Eros pleads with Zeus for Psyche, and eventually she and Eros are married.

This last task is really a journey, one that takes the individual face to face with death. This is the inner journey that results in transformation, but it is undertaken only with respect for the perils that can befall the unsuspecting traveler. Only love, or Eros, can save Psyche in the end from a sleep that is like death. As Johnson explains, "Only love can save you from the hardness and remoteness of partial spirituality."[4] Without love, we have a tendency to be self-righteous, to see ourselves as spiritually superior. Thus the warning to those who follow the narrow way of grief in divorce is to hold onto compassion and humility toward others, including your ex-spouse.

One thing that this final task highlights is the common pitfall on this journey of allowing oneself to be distracted by love. It is tempting to short circuit the journey of grief in divorce by entering into a romantic relationship. But as you have read in the stories presented in this book, this would deprive you of the gold that is waiting for you if you hold fast to your commitment.

What Psyche learned is that failure brings her victory. So, too, you will come to understand that the failure of your marriage—the loss of the image of perfection—has actually brought you to an experience of life that is greater than you could have previously imagined. This is the gold that will emerge from the fires of spiritual formation in the grief of divorce. By allowing yourself to be guided by your relationship with God in Christ and to surrender to what He is calling you to do—the tasks that lay before you—you will become the person you were created to be.

1. Take a few minutes to read the story of Eros and Psyche for yourself. An excellent book on this myth is *She* by Robert Johnson.[5] You can also find the story on the Internet. Prayerfully consider which tasks might be in front of you at this point in your journey. Identify those that seem the most difficult. Which aspects of your personality seem to be the most challenged by these tasks? If you like order and harmony, perhaps you're being challenged to develop a greater capacity for flexibility and openness. Or perhaps you have a tendency to be passive and unassertive and you're now being challenged to learn how to be more active in your life decisions. Write about this in your journal.

2. Though we can experience God in a number of ways, most of us have a preferred pathway to the Divine. Some people prefer to study the Bible and thus find an experience of God through

their intellect; others approach God through serving others and find their deepest connection to God through their relationships. Others find the contemplative approaches of centering prayer or Lectio Divina to be the most conducive toward an experience of the presence of God. Which of these do you most identify with? Which would you find least appealing? This week, consider practicing a different approach to God than the one you usually take. If you prefer acts of service, try a contemplative approach. If you prefer Bible study, try an act of service. Write about your experiences in your journal.

Conclusion

Teach me, O God, not to torture myself,
not to make a martyr out of myself
through stifling reflection,
but rather teach me to
breathe deeply in faith.
—Søren Kierkegaard

There comes a moment when people
who have been dabbling in religion
("man's search for God") suddenly draw back.
Supposing that we really found Him?
We never meant it to come to that!
Worse still, supposing He had found us?
—C.S. Lewis
Miracles

In writing this book, I have tried to mirror the journey of spiritual and emotional growth that can take place in the wake of divorce. Holding fast to the notion that God shows up in the darkest hours of our lives, we have explored the process of the grief of divorce, moving from confusion and despair into grief and sadness, and finally emerging into the possibility of a new experience of God, ourselves, and others. Along the way, we have heard the stories of individuals who have traversed this same pathway. Though unique in the details, each told of the journey from grief to transformation and of the surprising ways in which God revealed himself in the process. "Supposing that we really found Him?" asks C.S. Lewis. "We never meant it to come to that!"[1]

I think that what is so wonderful and amazing about God is how He reveals Himself in the most unexpected places and at the most unexpected times. I know in my own life, I've been privileged to experience God's presence during a therapy group in a psychiatric unit, a meeting with a student in my faculty office, and in the quiet of a silent moment with a client.

One of the most moving experiences I can remember of the real presence of grace occurred when I was an intern working in a behavioral medicine unit of a hospital. Though most of the time I was working with patients as a group therapist, on one occasion I was able to find an empty office to meet with a young woman in private.

She had been admitted that day after a psychotic episode and she was greatly distressed, not because of her psychosis as much as the condemnation she was experiencing from members of her church who felt that by coming into the hospital, she was not trusting in God to heal her. These were not Christians whose theology held to avoiding medical procedures. But when it comes to emotional and mental illness, some Christians put them in a different category, seeing them as a choice rather than an illness.

She and I talked awhile and though I cannot recall what I said, I do remember her words to me. After becoming slightly tearful, she confessed, "I never thought I'd find God's grace in a psych unit." In that moment I knew that God had shown up, and we were both touched by the encounter. As I later reflected to her, isn't that often the way it is with God? Where else but in a psychiatric unit would you expect to find God?

This is the truth about Christianity: It is, and always has been, a religion for the marginalized, for the outsiders, for those whom life has dealt an unfair blow. And eventually, we are all in that category. None of us gets through life without some measure of suffering. It is my hope that this book will encourage you to continue the journey with like-minded believers, fellow travelers on this journey of faith who don't have it all figured out but are willing to stumble forward nevertheless.

At the end of his book, *Blue Like Jazz*, Donald Miller describes the time he fell in love with Jesus: "I remember it was cold outside, crisp, and the leaves in the trees of the park across the street were getting tired and dry. And I remember sitting at my desk, and I don't know what it was that I read or what Jesus was doing in the book, but I felt a love for Him rush through me, through my back and into my chest."[2]

He goes onto say, "I think the most important thing that happens within Christian spirituality is when a person falls in love with Jesus."[3] That is my prayer for you. That you would find, or rediscover, or hold fast to, the love that you have for Jesus and let it carry you through the darkest hours of your life. I pray that you will allow God, through the Holy Spirit, to open you up to new insights, new understandings— in short a new vision of who God is, and who you are in Christ. Then you, too, can say that while you wouldn't choose to go through a divorce, you are grateful for the redemptive grace that has allowed you to be transformed in the process. Having experienced the vastness of God's grace, may you in turn pass that along to others. Blessings to you as you continue your journey.

1. Read through the journal you have kept during the time you have read this book. What changes do you see in yourself since you began? What has been the most significant insight you have gained? How do you see God's presence in your life now? Has your perspective changed? It what ways? Make a commitment to continue your journaling in the weeks and months to follow.

2. Read Isaiah 11:6–9. Consider how this might be a promise not only concerning the time when Christ will come again but also about the promise of your own inner life as you continue to cooperate with the Holy Spirit in your journey of spiritual formation. Read this passage prayerfully and ask the Holy Spirit to reveal something important—a word or a phrase that speaks directly to

you—in this moment. Read the passage through again and ask God to reveal a symbol or image that you can carry with you as you continue your journey. Make a visual representation of this image through drawing or find something that will remind you of this image. Take a moment to offer a prayer of gratitude.

Resources

As a psychotherapist, I am a big believer in the benefits of what my profession offers. My motto is that if we have to go through suffering, let's at least learn something from it. A well-trained licensed professional can assist you to learn and grow through times of struggle. Below are some resources to help you find a licensed professional in your area. I recommend that you interview prospective counselors by asking them a little about their training, their specialties, and their experience in working with divorced individuals. I'd suggest finding someone who is trained to look at family dynamics and who views challenges as opportunities for growth rather than as a mental illness. Below are national organizations and their websites.

American Association of Marriage and Family Therapists (AAMFT)

www.AAMFT.org

This is the national association for Marriage and Family Therapists with chapters in every state. Marriage and Family Therapists are trained to work with relationships. You can find a licensed professional in your area through their website or directly on www.TherapistLocator.net.

American Association of Christian Counselors (AACC)

www.aacc.net

This is a network of Christian Counselors who offer a variety of services. Many of their members are licensed professionals, though a large number are non-licensed coaches, lay counselors, or pastoral counselors.

American Psychological Association (APA)

www.apa.org

The APA is the most prominent association for psychologists and features an option to help you find a psychologist in your area. Psychologists have earned a doctorate in the field of psychology and many specialize in relational counseling as well.

American Counseling Association (ACA)

www.counseling.org

Members of the ACA are licensed professional counselors, most of whom are trained in short-term approaches. Just as with MFTs and Psychologists, look for someone who specializes in relational issues.

National Association of Social Workers (NASW)

www.socialworkers.org

Clinical social workers are a branch of the profession who specialize in assisting individuals with many personal challenges. The NASW website also features an option to assist you in finding a licensed professional in your area.

In addition to professional counselors, you may want to look into the services of a spiritual director. A spiritual director is not a counselor or psychotherapist, but someone who is trained to help you find the presence of God in your life, to answer the question, "Where is God showing up in this situation?" A qualified spiritual director will have had formal training in this process, during which time he or she learned to be a mentor to those seeking guidance in their spiritual walk. You can find a spiritual director in your area via the Internet. You also can find spiritual directors through training programs at various seminaries throughout the country.

Spiritual Directors International

www.sdiworld.org

This website offers additional information on spiritual direction and hosts an option for locating a spiritual director in your area. Be sure to look for a director that works in the Christian tradition, as not all of those listed in the directory are Christians.

Recommended Reading

The following is a list of books that have either been referenced in this book or have been helpful to my clients and others in their spiritual walk.

Companions in Christ (Upper Room Books)

This is a series that you can study on your own, or preferably, with others. The series introduces readers to the ideas of spiritual formation within the context of ancient and modern Christian writers and thinkers. I recommend this as a way to continue the journey you have begun in reading this book.

Longing for God (2009) Richard J. Foster and Gayle D. Beebe

This book explores the seven paths to Christian devotion through the lives of Christian writers who have eloquently explored diverse and multifaceted responses to God. This offers the reader an opportunity to learn about the depth and richness of Christianity within the context of a modern faith journey.

Soul Making (1989) Alan Jones

In a similar fashion to Foster and Beebe, Jones takes the reader on a journey into the ancient spirituality of Christianity. He focuses more exclusively on the ideas of the desert fathers and mothers—those early Christians who sought an experience of God by physically separating from daily human contact. Jones shows how it is possible to rediscover the sense of mystery and awe that is sometimes lacking in modern Christian experience.

The End of the World as We Know It (2001) Chuck Smith, Jr.

This thought-provoking work challenges readers to examine modern Christianity within the context of the idea of spiritual community. Smith takes readers on a tour of post-modern assumptions and how these present both a challenge and an opportunity to Christians to remain a vital and much-needed influence in the world.

The Divine Conspiracy (1998) Dallas Willard

To say that this book explores what it means to really be a disciple of Christ is an understatement, but it is the most succinct description I could come up with for a work that has influenced so many individuals. This is a book that would create a wonderful centerpiece for a small group of like-minded seekers.

In the Twinkle of an "I" (2008) Daniel L. Tocchini

Tocchini offers the reader an opportunity to challenge the notion that purpose and meaning in life are something to be achieved and instead presents the idea that Christian spirituality is inherently about a principled and values-driven life.

Inner Work (1990) Robert A. Johnson

I highly recommend any of Johnson's works (*We: Understanding the Psychology of Romantic Love* is particularly helpful in understanding the power of romance), but this book is one of the most useful for those interested in exploring dreams.

Sacred Romance (1997) Brent Curtis and John Eldridge

Drawing near to the heart of God is the longing of every Christian. This book leads the reader into a deeper examination of what this means and an understanding that the desire for a transcendent love belongs only within the context of the divine.

A New Kind of Christian (2001) Brian D. McLaren

McLaren uses a parable to take the reader on a journey through some of the current challenges and opportunities that confront the Christian faith. It is an opportunity to discern the way in which the Holy Spirit is moving the church into the twenty-first century as a significant and living force.

Notes

Introduction

1. William Least Heat-Moon, *Blue Highways: A journey into America* (Boston: Little Brown and Company, 1982) p. 5.
2. ibid., p. 411.
3. W.H. Auden, *Auden Poems*, E. Mendelson, Ed. (New York: Alfred A. Knopf, 1995) p. 50.
4. ibid.
5. Anne Rice, *The Queen of the Damned* (New York, Ballantine Books: 1988), p. 62.
6. D.H. Lawrence, *Complete Poems*, V. Sol Pinto and W. Roberts, Eds. (New York: Penguin Books, 1993) p. 109.
7. Clarissa Pinkola Estes, *Women Who Run with the Wolves: Myths and Stories of the Wild Woman Archetype* (New York: Ballantine Books, 1992).

Chapter One

1. Susan Spano, "An Historical Romance," in *Women on Divorce*, P. Kaganoff and S. Spano, Eds. (New York: Harcourt Brace and Company, 1995), p. 134.
2. James Fenhagen, *Invitation to Holiness* (San Francisco: Harper & Row, 1985), p. 10.

Chapter Two

1. Marion Woodman, *Addiction to Perfection: The Still Unravished Bride* (Toronto: Inner City Books, 1982).

Chapter Three

1. C.S. Lewis, *A Grief Observed* (New York: Bantam Books, 1963), p. 1.
2. Alan Paton, *For You Departed* (New York: Charles Scribner's Sons, 1969), p. 8.
3. Geoffrey Gorer, *Death, Grief and Mourning: A study of Contemporary Society* (New York: Doubleday, 1965), p. 131.
4. John Bowlby, *Loss: Sadness and Depression* (New York: Basic Books, 1980), p. 7.

5. Abigail Trafford, *Crazy Time: Surviving Divorce* (New York: Bantam Books, 1982), p. 43.
6. Stephanie Ericsson, *Companion Through the Darkness: Inner Dialogues on Grief* (New York: HarperCollins, 1993), p. 84.
7. Lynne Caine, *Widow: The Personal Crisis of a Widow in America* (New York: William Morris & Co., 1974), p. 92.
8. Rollo May, *The Courage to Create* (New York: W.W. Norton & Company, 1975).
9. Kathleen Norris, *The Psalms* (New York: Riverhead Books, 1997), p. vii.

Chapter Four

1. Patrick Henry, *The Ironic Christian's Companion: Finding the Marks of God's Grace in the World* (New York: Riverhead Books, 1999), p. 7.
2. David Wolpe, Making Loss Matter: Creating Meaning in Difficult Times (New York: Riverhead Books, 1999), p. 6.
3. *The Spiritual Formation Bible: Growing in Intimacy with God through the Scriptures.* The New International Version (Grand Rapids, MI: Zondervan Publishing, 1999), p. 689.

Chapter Five

1. Henri J. M. Nouwen, *Here and Now* (New York: Crossroad Publishing, 1994), p. 145.

Chapter Six

1. Aldo Carotenuto, *To Love to Betray: Life as Betrayal*, J. Tambureno, trans., (Wilmette, IL: Chiron Publications, 1996). Original work published 1991.
2. Anne Wilson Schaef, *Co-dependence: Misunderstood—Mistreated*, (San Francisco: Harper & Row Publishers, 1986), p. 48.
3. Marilyn Jensen, *Formerly Married: Learning to Live with Yourself* (New York: Westminster Press, 1977), p. 116.
4. Sean O'Reilly, James O'Reilly, and Tim O'Reilly, Eds., *The Road Within: True Stories of Transformation* (San Francisco: Traveler's Tales, Inc., 1997), p. xvii.
5. ibid.

Chapter Seven

1. Ted Solotaroff, "Getting the Point," in Peggy Kaganoff and Susan Spano (Eds.), *Men on Divorce: The Other Side of the Story* (New York: Harcourt Brace and Company, 1997), p. 28.
2. Thomas Jones, *The Single Again Handbook: Finding Meaning and Fulfillment When You're Single Again* (Nashville, TN: Thomas Nelson Publishers, 1993), p. xii.
3. Mary Lou Redding, *Breaking and Mending: Divorce and God's Grace* (Nashville, TN: Upper Room Books, 1998), p. 17.

4. John Bradshaw, *Healing the Shame that Binds You* (Deerfield Beach, FL: Health Communications, Inc., 1988).
5. Ernest Kurtz, *Shame & Guilt* (New York: IUniverse, Inc., 2007).
6. *The Twelve Steps: A Spiritual Journey* (San Diego, CA: RPI Publishing Inc., 1994), pp. x–xi.
7. Mary Lou Redding, *Breaking and Mending: Divorce and God's Grace*, p. 67.
8. ibid., pp. 67-68.
9. ibid., p. 69.

Chapter Eight
1. Edward Edinger, *The Bible and the Psyche: Individuation Symbolism in the Old Testament* (Toronto: Inner City Books, 1986), p. 41.

Chapter Nine
1. David Schnarch, *Passionate Marriage: Love, Sex and Intimacy in Emotionally Committed Relationships* (New York: W.W. Norton & Company, 1997).
2. Dr. Seuss, *The Sneetches and Other Stories* (New York: Random House, 1961), p. 50.

Chapter Ten
1. John Sanford, *Dreams: God's Forgotten Language* (San Francisco: HarperSanFrancisco, 1989), p. 82.
2. ibid.
3. John Sanford, *The Kingdom Within: The Inner Meanings of Jesus' Sayings* (San Francisco: HarperSanFrancisco, 1987), p. 23.
4. John Sanford, *Dreams: God's Forgotten Language*, p. 14
5. Robert Johnson, *Inner Work: Using Dreams & Active Imagination for Personal Growth* (San Francisco: HarperSanFrancisco, 1986).

Chapter Eleven
1. Alan Jones, *Soul Making: The Desert Way of Spirituality* (San Francisco: HarperSanFrancisco, 1989), p. 45.

Chapter Twelve
1. James Hillman, *Suicide and the Soul* (Dallas, TX: Spring Publications, Inc., 1965), p. 15.
2. James Hillman, *Suicide and the Soul,* p. 63.
3. Robert Johnson, *She: Understanding Feminine Psychology,* (San Francisco: HarperSanFrancisco, 1989).

4. ibid., p. 72.

5. ibid.

Conclusion

1. C.S. Lewis, *Miracles: A Preliminary Study,* (New York: Harper Collins, 1947), p. 60.

2. Donald Miller, *Blue Like Jazz: Nonreligious Thoughts on Christian Spirituality* (Nashville, TN: Thomas Nelson Publishers, 2003), p. 237.

3. ibid.

Additional References

Auden, W.H. *Auden Poems.* New York: Alfred A. Knopf, 1995.

Bowlby, John. *Loss: Sadness and Depression.* New York: Basic Books, 1980.

Bradshaw, John. *Healing the Shame that Binds You.* Deerfield, FL: Health Communications, Inc., 1988.

Caine, Lynne. *Widow: The Personal Crisis of a Widow in America.* New York: William Morris & Co., 1974.

Carotenuto, Aldo. *To Love to Betray: Life as Betrayal, J. Tambureno, trans.* Wilmette, IL.: Chiron Publications, 1991. Original work published 1991.

Edinger, Edward. *The Bible and the Psyche: Individuation Symbolism in the Old Testament.* Toronto: Inner City Books, 1986.

Ericsson, Stephanie. *Companion Through the Darkness: Inner Dialogues on Grief.* New York: HaperCollins, 1993.

Estes, Clarissa Pinkola. *Women Who Run With the Wolves.* New York: Ballantine Books, 1992.

Fenhagin, James. *Invitation to Holiness.* San Francisco: Harper & Row, 1985.

Gorer, Geoffrey. *Death, Grief and Mourning: A Study of Contemporary Society.* New York: Doubleday, 1965.

Heat-Moon, William Least. *Blue Highways.* Boston: Little, Brown and Company, 1982.

Henry, Patrick. *The Ironic Christian's Companion: Finding the Marks of God's Grace in the World.* New York: Riverhead Books, 1999.

Hillman, James. *Suicide and the Soul.* Dallas, TX: Spring Publications, Inc., 1965.

Jensen, Marilyn. *Formerly Married: Learning to Live With Yourself.* New York: Westminster Press, 1977.

Johnson, Robert. *Inner Work.* San Francisco: HarperSanFrancisco, 1986.

—. *She: Understanding Feminine Psychology.* San Francisco: HarperSanFrancisco, 1989.

Jones, Alan. *Soul Making: The Desert Way of Spirituality.* San Francisco: HarperSanFrancisco, 1989.

Jones, Thomas. *The Single Again Handbook: Finding Meaning and Fulfillment When You're Single Again.* Nashville, TN: Thomas Nelson Publishers, 1993.

Kurtz, Ernest. *Shame and Guilt.* New York: iUniverse, Inc., 2007.

Lawrence, D.H. *Complete Poems.* New York: Penguin Books, 1993.

Lewis, C.S. *Miracles: A Preliminary Study.* New York: Harper Collins, 1947.

—. *A Grief Observed.* New York: Bantam Books, 1963.

Miller, Donald. *Blue Like Jazz: Nonreligious Thoughts on Christian Spirituality.* Nashville, TN: Thomas Nelson Publishers, 2003.

Norris, Kathleen. *The Psalms.* New York: Riverhead Books, 1997.

Nouwen, Henri J.M. *Here and Now.* New York: Crossroad Publishing, 1994.

Paton, Alan. *For You Departed.* New York: Charles Scribner's Sons, 1969.

Redding, Mary Lou. *Breaking and Mending: Divorce and God's Grace.* Nashville, TN: Upper Room Books, 1998.

Rice, Anne. *The Queen of the Damned.* New York: Ballantine Books, 1988.

RPI Publishing, Inc. *The Twelve Steps: A Spiritual Journey.* San Diego, CA: RPI Publishing, Inc., 1994.

Sanford, John. *Dreams: God's Forgotten Language.* San Francisco: Harper-SanFrancisco, 1989.

—. *The Kingdom Within: The Inner Meaning of Jesus' Sayings.* San Francisco: HarperSanFrancisco, 1987.

Schaef, Anne Wilson. *Co-dependence: Misunderstood—Mistreated.* San Francisco: Harper & Row Publishers, 1986.

Schnarch, David. *Passionate Marriage: Love, Sex and Intimacy in Emotionally Committed Relationships.* New York: W.W. Norton & Company, 1997.

Sean O'Reilly, James O'Reilly and Tim O'Reilly, Eds. *The Road Within: True Stories of Transformation.* San Francisco: Travelers Tales, Inc., 1997.

Seuss, Dr. *The Sneetches and Other Stories.* New York: Random House, 1961.

Solotaroff, Ted. "Getting the Point" *in P. Kaganoff and S. Spano, Eds., Men on Divorce.* New York: Harcourt Brace and Company, 1995.

Spano, Susan. "An Historial Romance" *in P. Kaganoff and S. Spano, Eds. Women on Divorce.* New York: Harcourt Brace and Company, 1995.

Trafford, Abigail. *Crazy Time: Surviving Divorce.* New York: Bantam Books, 1982.

Willard, Dallas. *The Divine Conspiracy: Rediscovering Our Hidden Life in God.* New York: HarperOne, 1997.

Woodman, Marion. *Addiction to Perfection: The Still Unravished Bride.* Toronto: Inner City Books, 1982.